Life Styles

STUDENT'S BOOK 2

FRANCISCO LOZANO

JANE STURTEVANT

Project Coordinator: Lyn McLean
Developmental Editor: Larry Anger
Consultants: Russell N. Campbell and William E. Rutherford

LIFE STYLES, Student's Book 2

3 4 5 6 7 8 9 10 AL 95949392

ISBN: 0 582 79757 8

Library of Congress Catalog Card Number: 82–78

Project Editor: **Annica Davis**
Character Illustrations: **M. J. Quay**
Cover Design: **Frederick Charles Ltd.**
Cover Photography: **Dorien Grunbaum** and **Redmond Johnston**
Design: **Cris Graña**
Production Manager: **Anne Musso**
Photo/Art Credits: See page 121

Printed in the U.S.A.

Longman Inc.
19 West 44th Street
New York, New York 10036
U.S.A.

Instituto Mexicano Norteamericano
de Relaciones Culturales, A. C.
Hamburgo 115
México 6, D. F.

Acknowledgments

We wish to thank
  Oscar Castro
  Victoria Kimbrough
for leading the way;
  Luis Abreu
  John Stering
for field-testing the materials;
  Mary Martin
  Lois McKeon
  Alicia Valenzuela
for helping prepare the manuscript;
  Ignazio Amero
for illustrating the pilot edition;
  Brian Abbs
  Ingrid Freebairm
for allowing us to adapt the Language Summary from *Starting Strategies* (Longman Group Ltd., London 1978).

Finally, we wish to acknowledge the cooperation of the teaching, administrative and editorial staffs of the Instituto Mexicano Norteamericano de Relaciones Culturales and Longman New York, and thank the friends and family members who encouraged and supported us.

Francisco Lozano
Jane Sturtevant

New York and Mexico, 1982

Contents

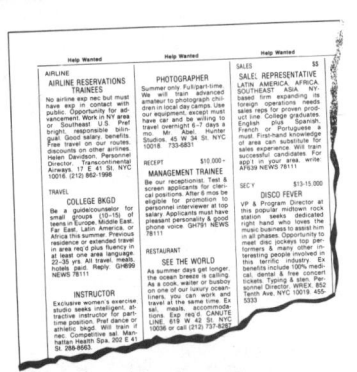

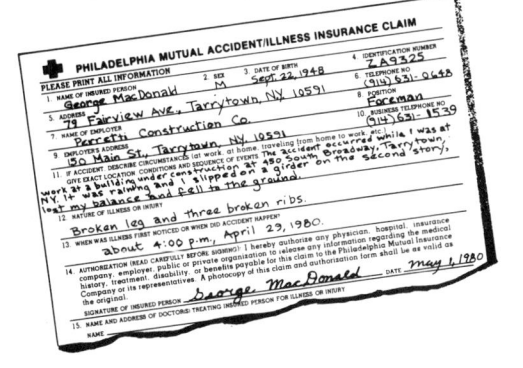

UNIT 1 I'm having a party for my boyfriend.

Mac's birthday's Saturday and I'm having a surprise party for him.

Maria Sanchez is in the Hotel Management Program at New York University. As part of her program, she works at the Regency Hotel in New York. She's having a surprise party for her boyfriend. During a break at work, she's calling people to invite them to the party.

Could we meet at your apartment?

Of course.

Paula Duran is a reporter for the *New York News*. She lives next door to Mac. Originally she's from Chicago.

Paula's coming. Can you? We're going to meet at her apartment at about quarter to eight.

Sure. I'll be there. Thanks for asking me.

Ray Palmer and Paula Duran have been seeing each other for several months. He's a sales <u>representative</u> for a large manufacturing company in New York. He's a widower and his two children live with their grandparents in Atlanta.

What a nice idea! Who else are you inviting?

Probably Tomiko Sato and some of our other friends from school.

George and Maggie MacDonald and their son, Billy, live in Tarrytown, a small town near New York City. George is Mac's older brother. He's a foreman for a construction company. Maggie and Paula Duran have been friends since they went to college together in Chicago.

I'd like to take you out to dinner Saturday for your birthday. Is eight o'clock all right?

OK. I'll pick you up at eight.

Hey, that's great! Sure, eight o'clock's fine.

Mac (his real name is Keith) MacDonald is going to be 25 on Saturday. He's in the engineering program at Columbia University and he's getting his degree in June.

Fill in the missing information			
Name	Occupation	Place of Work and/or School	Marital Status
Mac MacDonald			
	housewife		
		Regency Hotel NYU	
		construction company	
			widower
	not given	not given	not given
Tomiko Sato			
	reporter		single

What does Maggie want to tell Paula?
Why are George and Maggie going to Paula's early?
√ Does Maggie tell Paula where she's going to go to school?

On the morning of Mac's birthday, Maggie called Paula.

"Is everything all set for the party?" asked Maggie.

"Yeah. Maria called a little while ago and said everyone would be here by quarter to eight. She's really excited."

"Well, I hope Mac's surprised. She's worked awfully hard to organize this thing." *very really*

"Yeah, she has. So what's new with *you*?"

"Well, as a matter of fact I *do* have something to tell you. I've decided to go back to school."

"You're kidding! What happened? I thought you wanted to open a sporting goods store."

· "Yeah, well, when I first talked to you about it, it seemed like a good idea, but . . . well, I just wasn't being very realistic. First I've got to learn something about running a business. Anyway, I'm really excited about going to school again. I've been getting information about colleges in the area and some of them—"

"Oh, there's the doorbell," interrupted Paula. "I have to go. Ray's picking me up so we can go shopping. Listen, why don't you and George come early tonight so we have a chance to talk before the party? Say, six or six thirty?"

"OK. We'll try to get there by six thirty. Say hi to Ray."

Paula and Ray had agreed to meet downstairs in front of Paula's apartment building so Ray wouldn't have to look for a place to park. After she said goodbye to Maggie, Paula grabbed her jacket and hurried down to the car.

"Hi," she said. "Sorry I took so long. I was just talking to Maggie."

"Oh, yeah? How is she?"

"She's fine. She said they'd try to get here around six thirty so we can talk for a while before everybody starts arriving."

"Oh, that's a good idea. What else did she have to say?"

"You won't believe it. She said she's decided to go back to school."

"No kidding! That certainly takes courage. I wish her luck. Did she tell you what she wants to study?"

"No, and I didn't have time to ask her. I guess she'll tell us tonight."

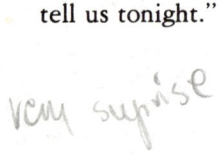

very suprise

he, she say – said | SUBJECT
her, them tell – told | OBJECT
UNIT ONE 3

1. CONVERSATION. Greet someone and tell him/her what's new with you.

> To tell someone what's new, you can tell them about something:
>
> you did recently: I just talked to Paula.
> you've decided to do: I've decided (not) to open a store.
> you're going to do: I'm going back to school.

A: Hi, ... How are you?
B: I'm fine How are you?
A: I'm fine. So what's new with you?
B: Well, as a matter of fact, I do have something to tell you. .... OR Oh, nothing much. ....
A/B: (*Continue the conversation.*)

2. CONVERSATION. Tell someone about your conversation above. Report what your friend told you.

A: I was just talking to *her*. *He/She* said................
B: Did *he/she* tell you ....? *what*
A: ....
B: What else did *he/she* have to say?
A: ....

> *You can say:*
>
> Did she tell you { what she's taking?
> where she's going?
> who she went with?
> where it was?

3. GRAMMAR FOCUS. Fill in the blanks with the appropriate form of *say* or *tell*.

PAULA: I talked to Maria this morning. She
 .....said.....₁ she needs more glasses for
 tonight. Do you have any we can use?
RAY: Sure. .....Tell.....₂ her I can bring about ten.
PAULA: OK, good.
RAY: Did she .....say.....₃ what time everybody
 would be arriving?
PAULA: Yeah, she .....said.....₄ she .....told.....₅ them to
 get here by quarter to eight.

4. 🎞 **LISTENING.** Maria called Paul Mitchell, an old college friend of Mac's who has just moved to New York from St. Louis. These are the notes Paul wrote while Maria was talking. Listen to their conversation and fill in the blanks.

> __7:40__ p.m.
> __688__ Columbus Ave. Apt. __3 G__
> __F__ train to Atlantic Ave.
> Change to # __2 or 3__ Express.
> Get off at __9 6__.

A new kind of student

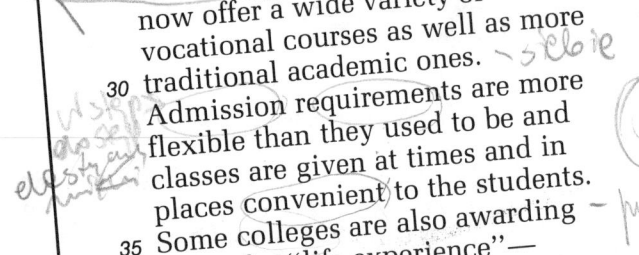

Stanley Danzis has been a lumberjack for the last five years working in the forests of Oregon and Washington. Since last
5 September, he has also been a college student. "I figure by the time I'm about 35, I'll be ready to take it easy—ready for a little more comfort than you find in the woods.
10 I've always thought I'd like to teach kindergarten, so I'm going to get a degree in education."

Stanley Danzis is representative of the fastest-growing group of
15 students in the country. By 1985, the Census Bureau estimates forty percent of all college students will be over 25. Why are so many adults going to college? Most of them
20 hope to get better jobs or like Stanley to change careers.

Because the nation now has fewer 18-to-21-year-olds than it used to have, colleges are over-
25 expanded. They need more students and they are going out of their way to attract adults. Colleges now offer a wide variety of vocational courses as well as more
30 traditional academic ones. Admission requirements are more flexible than they used to be and classes are given at times and in places convenient to the students.
35 Some colleges are also awarding credit for "life experience"— what people have learned at work or in their personal lives.

This is all well and good,
40 except for the problem of financial aid. Almost all loans and scholar-ships are reserved for full-time students, while most returning adults study part time. For poor
45 students the problems are enormous.

Linda Tyler is one of those students who cannot get financial aid. Married at 18 and divorced at
50 23, she is now 25 and the mother of two preschool children. "My sister can only take care of the kids after she gets home from work, so I can't go to school full time." As a part-
55 time student, she is not eligible for aid. Her ex-husband helps her very little, so she lives on public assistance ("welfare") payments from the government. "If I can just
60 finish and get my degree, I'll be able to get a decent job and get off welfare, but sometimes I wonder if I'll be able to do it."

As more adults return to
65 school, laws may change so that more of these students will be eligible for financial aid. In the meantime, however, the people who need education the most are
70 the ones who have the hardest time getting it.

Many college teachers are unhappy because they feel that the college degree is losing its
75 traditional value. However, to most older students the degree isn't important anyway. It's only as good as the job it can get them. As one 28-year-old student says,
80 "It was only the hope of getting a better job that made me go back to school."

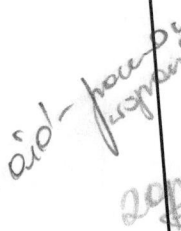

5. READING STRATEGY: Getting the meaning from context.

1. In paragraph 3 find a way to say "colleges have too many teachers, buildings, etc."

   Colleges are _____ over expended _____.

2. In paragraph 4 find three ways to say "money to pay for school."

   ....

   ....

   ....

3. Find a word in paragraph 5 that means "public assistance."

   welfare

4. Find an expression (four words) in paragraph 5 that means "Linda Tyler cannot get . . ."

   is not eligible for

   → the undifinje se

6. READING STRATEGY: Finding specific information. First circle *true* or *false*. Then underline the information in the article that shows your answer is right.

T (F)

1. Stanley Danzis works in a large city.

   > Stanley Danzis has been a lumberjack for the last five years underline{working in the forests of Oregon and Washington}. Since last September, he has also been a . . .

2. Today there are not very many adults who want to go back to college. T (F)
3. Colleges are trying to get more adults to go back to school. T (F)
4. It's easy for most returning students to get money for college. T (F)
5. Most older students are back in school because they like to study and learn. T (F)

7. READING STRATEGY: Finding specific information. Circle the correct answers. (There may be more than one correct answer.)

1. Stanley Danzis is
   a. a lumberjack.
   b. a college student.
   c. a kindergarten teacher.
2. Linda Tyler hopes to
   a. get her degree, then get a job, then get off welfare.
   b. get a job and get off welfare, then get her degree.
   c. get off welfare first, then get her degree and get a job.
3. Colleges now offer
   a. good jobs.
   b. traditional academic courses.
   c. vocational courses.

Why does Maggie want to take business courses?
What kind of school is Maggie looking for?
What does Paula think about Fordham?

When Maggie and George got to Paula's, Ray was already there. Paula took them into the living room.

"So what's this about going back to school?" Paula asked Maggie. "Are you really serious?"

"Yeah, I've decided to go back and take some business courses."

"Why business?" asked Ray.

"Well, because I want to have a store someday. But first I need to know something about retailing. Right now, I wouldn't know where to begin."

"Have you decided where you want to go?" asked Paula.

"No, not yet, but I've been thinking about Fordham. I'd like to go someplace where there are students my age."

"Well, from what I've heard, Fordham has one of the best programs around here for returning students."

"It's pretty far from Tarrytown, though," said George.

"Yeah, it is, but I don't mind driving."

"Well, I'm really impressed," said Ray.

"So am I," said George. "I couldn't do it."

Paula raised her glass. "Here's to you, Maggie. Good luck."

---

8.   CONVERSATION. Talk about a change you want to make in your life (*change jobs/get a job/change schools/go back to school/move*).

A: *I've decided to* ....*/I think I might* ....

B: Really? Why?

A: Because I *want to/need to/have to* ....

B: Have you decided where you want to *work/go/live?*

A: No, not yet, but I've been thinking about .... I'd like to .... someplace where ....

B: That's a good idea.   OR   How about ....? (*From what I've heard,*) *it's/it has* one of the .... *around here/in town/in the area/in the country.*

Here are some reasons for choosing a place:

I'd like to work someplace where they pay more.
I'd like to go someplace where there are students my age.
I'd like to live someplace where I can walk to work.

GRAMMAR NOTE:

Valhalla is **the biggest** college (in the area).
It's one of **the most expensive** colleges (in the area.)
It's one of **the least attractive** colleges (around here).
Duke College has one of **the best** nursing programs (in the area).
Duke College has one of **the worst** business programs (around here).
It's **the farthest** from my house.

9. GRAMMAR FOCUS.
Using the chart, fill in the blanks in the conversation with items from the list. Use each item only once.

- the most
- the best
- the cheapest
- the biggest
- the closest

COMPARISON OF COLLEGES	Undergraduate enrollment	Part-time enrollment	Degrees offered	Tuition and fees (part-time)	Special classes	Facilities for returning students		
						Special counseling	Financial aid	Credit for life experience
Valhalla Community College, Valhalla	6,858	2,090	AA	$ 500	✓	✓	✓	✓
State University, Pleasantville	2,209	696	AA BA	$2,430	—	✓	—	✓
Grover College, Tarrytown	910	12	BA	$1,200	—	—	—	—
Duke College, New Rochelle	3,112	848	AA BA	$2,000	—	✓	✓	✓
White Plains Community College, White Plains	4,453	1,120	AA	$ 800	—	✓		

MAGGIE: Look. Here's something that gives information about colleges near Tarrytown that have part-time programs.

PAULA: Oh, let me see. . . . Well, Grover College is certainly _the closest_ —it's right there in Tarrytown.

MAGGIE: Yeah, but they don't have any facilities for returning students. Anyway, I'd like to go to a bigger school than that.

PAULA: Well, Valhalla Community College is _the biggest_ one of these five, and I see it also has _the most_ part-time students.

MAGGIE: Yeah, but it doesn't offer a B.A. White Plains Community College doesn't either.

PAULA: Oh, that's too bad. They're _the cheapest_ ones too.

MAGGIE: I know. The others are a lot more expensive. And look at what Valhalla offers for returning students.

PAULA: Oh, yeah. I see what you mean. It's really got _the best_ program, hasn't it?

10. READING STRATEGY: Getting the meaning from context.

1. According to the ad, EXCEL is
   a. a university
   b. a special program for adult students
   c. a special library at Fordham University.

2. EXCEL is for people who want to
   a. get a college degree.
   b. have a good time in school.
   c. take a few courses.

3. A *B.A.* is
   a. a degree.
   b. a course.
   c. financial aid.

4. An *undergraduate* is
   a. a student who is studying to get a B.A.
   b. a student who already has a B.A.
   c. a counselor for older students.

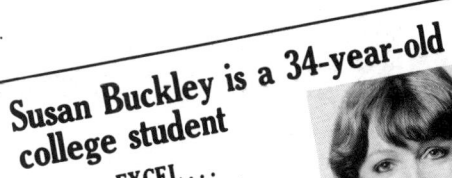

Was Maria planning to invite Anita to the party?
Is everyone meeting at Mac's or at Paula's?
What's the address?
How's Anita getting there?

The day of the party, Maria was about to leave work and go pick up the birthday cake she had ordered, when Anita Davis, a co-worker of hers, came looking for her.

ANITA: Hi, Maria. Hey, I really like your hair.
MARIA: Oh, thanks. I thought it was time for a change.
ANITA: It really looks great.
MARIA: Thanks.
ANITA: Say, I just found out I don't have to work tonight. Want to go to a movie?
MARIA: As a matter of fact, I'm having a surprise party for my boyfriend tonight. It's his birthday. Why don't you come?
ANITA: Oh, I don't know . . .
MARIA: Oh, come on. I'd like you to meet Mac. And he's got some cute friends. It'll be fun.

ANITA: Well, all right. Thank you. What time?
MARIA: We're meeting at his neighbor's apartment at quarter to eight.
ANITA: OK. Where is it?
MARIA: 688 Columbus, at 94th St.
ANITA: I live in Greenwich Village. What's the best way to get there?
MARIA: Take the Seventh Avenue subway and get off at 96th Street. Then just walk two blocks to Columbus.
ANITA: OK. What was the address again? I'd better write it down.
MARIA: It's 688 Columbus Avenue. Apartment 3G. The name's Duran.
ANITA: OK. Thanks for inviting me.
MARIA: I'm glad you can come.

11. CONVERSATION. Invite someone to your house and tell him/her how to get there.

A:

Invite **B** to a party.

B:

Accept the invitation. Ask where **A** lives or where the party's going to be.

Answer.

Ask for directions:
I live .... What's the best way to get there?

Give directions:
Take the .... and get off at ....
Then walk .... blocks to ....

Confirm the address:
OK. What was the address again? I'd better write it down.

Give your address.

12. WRITING SKILLS. On her way to the party, Maria mailed a letter to a friend in Boston who was coming to stay with her for a couple of days.

Write a letter like Maria's. Tell your friend how to get to your house from the bus station, the railroad station or the airport. Include a map.

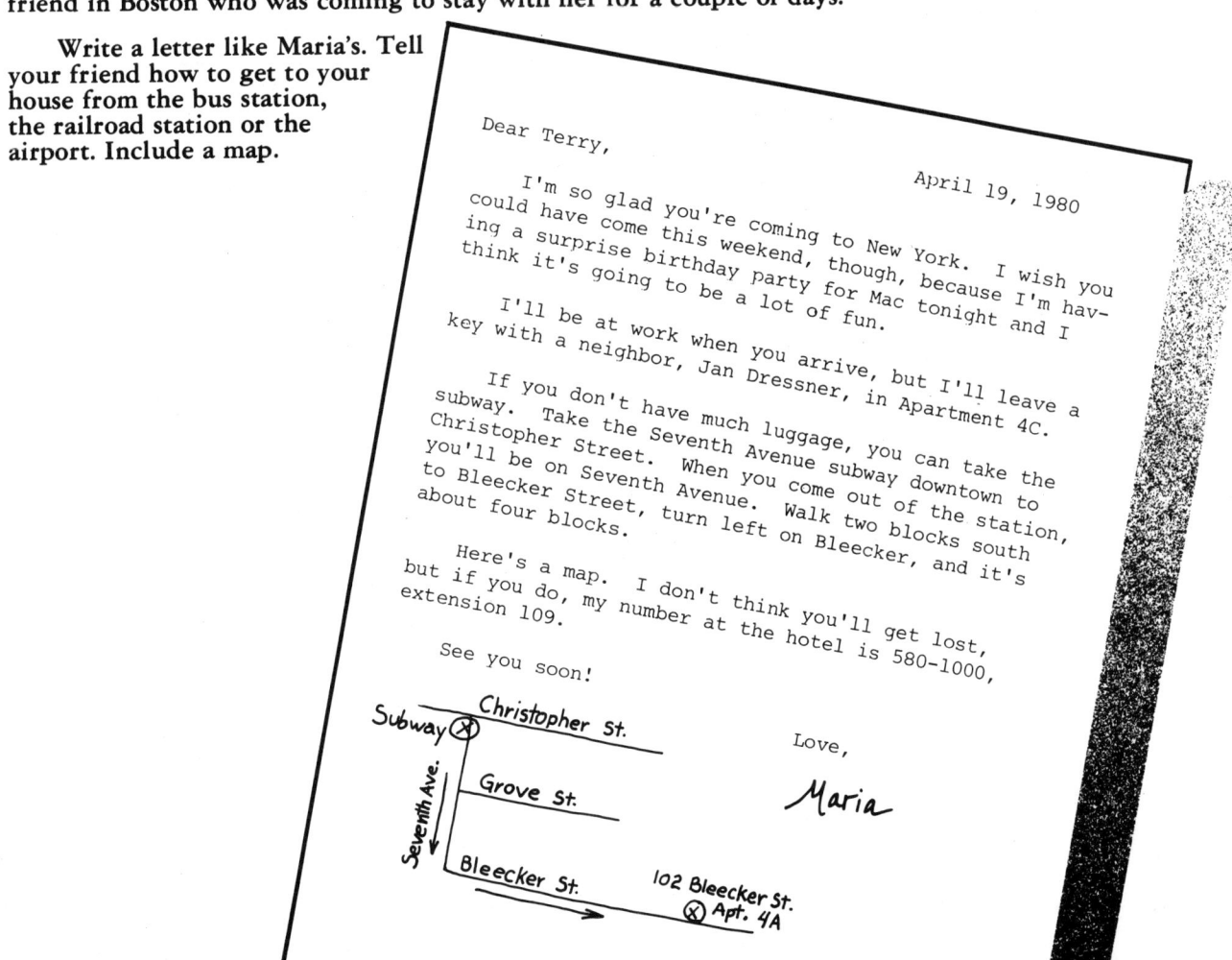

Dear Terry,

April 19, 1980

I'm so glad you're coming to New York. I wish you could have come this weekend, though, because I'm having a surprise birthday party for Mac tonight and I think it's going to be a lot of fun.

I'll be at work when you arrive, but I'll leave a key with a neighbor, Jan Dressner, in Apartment 4C.

If you don't have much luggage, you can take the subway. Take the Seventh Avenue subway downtown to Christopher Street. When you come out of the station, you'll be on Seventh Avenue. Walk two blocks south to Bleecker Street, turn left on Bleecker, and it's about four blocks.

Here's a map. I don't think you'll get lost, but if you do, my number at the hotel is 580-1000, extension 109.

See you soon!

Love,

Maria

REVIEW

YOU'VE LEARNED TO

start a conversation:	Hi, Paula. How are you?
	OK. So what's new with *you*?
emphasize:	Well, as a matter of fact, I *do* have something to tell you.
talk about a decision:	I've decided to go back to school./I'm going back to school.
	Really? Why?
	Because I need to know something about retailing.
	Have you decided where you want to go?
	No, not yet, but I've been thinking about Fordham.
report a conversation:	I was just talking to Maggie. She said she's decided to go back to school.
ask for further information:	Did she tell you what she wants to study?/What else did she have to say?
make a suggestion:	How about Fordham? From what I've heard, it has one of the best programs around here for returning students.
invite someone to do something:	I'm having a surprise party for my boyfriend tonight. Why don't you come?
ask for and give directions:	Where is it?
	688 Columbus, at 94th St.
	I live in Greenwich Village. What's the best way to get there?
	Take the Seventh Avenue subway and get off at 96th Street.
ask someone to repeat something:	What was the address again?

GRAMMAR

Say and Tell

> She **said** (that)* she's decided to go back to school.
> She **told me** (that) she's decided to go back to school.

* **That** is sometimes omitted, especially in conversation.

Just

> I was **just** talking to Maggie.

Embedded Questions

> Did she say / Did she tell you 〔 what she's taking? / where she's going? / who he went with? 〕

Relative Clause: **Where**

> I'd like to go someplace **where there are students my age.**

Superlative

> Valhalla is **the biggest** college (in the area).
> It's one of **the most expensive** colleges (in the area).
> It's one of **the least attractive** colleges (around here).
> Duke College has one of **the best** nursing programs (in the area).
> Duke College has one of **the worst** business programs (around here).
> It's **the farthest** from my house.

USEFUL WORDS AND EXPRESSIONS

get off	•	best	•
go back	age	•	as a matter of fact,
heard (hear)*	area	because	From what I've heard,
need	block	just	Nothing much.
pay	town	someplace	not yet
said (say)	way	•	So what's new with you?
write down	•	around	

* When an irregular form of a word appears in the units, the base form of the word is given in parentheses.

meany — more than — the most

1. CONVERSATION. You and your partner have just run into each other on the street. You haven't seen each other for a couple of months.

A:

> Greet **B** and ask what's new.

B:

> Tell **A** about a decision you've made which will change your life.

> Ask **B** for more information about his/her decision. Offer a suggestion that you think will help **B**.

> Continue the conversation.

2. GRAMMAR. A few weeks before, Maria had read a magazine article criticizing New York City. She didn't agree with what the article said and decided to write to the editor. — *redalulon, nydenne* **Fill in the blanks in her letter with the superlative form of words.**

LETTERS TO THE EDITOR:

We have received many letters about our recent article (April 21) on the problems of living in New York. Most of them agree with our report, but here is one that defends the Big Apple.

I certainly do *not* agree that New York is one of **the most difficult** [1. difficult] cities in the world to live in, and I don't think that New Yorkers are **the most unfriendly** [2. unfriendly] people in the U.S. either. People are always saying negative things about New York, and they always overlook the *positive* side. Here are a few facts your article did not mention:

- New York is truly a cultural center and is one of **the most exciting** [3. exciting] cities in the world today.
- It has **the most** [4. many] theaters of any city in the U.S. and its orchestras and dance companies are **the best** [5. good] in the country.
- New York has several of **the best** [6. fine] museums in the world—and New Yorkers actually go to them.

- New York has **the best** [7. great] variety of restaurants in the country. There are so many different kinds that they have to be listed by nationality in the telephone directory.
- New York's subway may not be **the most** [8. new] or **the cleanest** [9. clean] in the world, but it's probably one of **the most efficient** [10. efficient]

All of this makes New York a wonderful place to live, but **the most fascino** [11. fascinating] thing about this city is its people. They are **the most friendly** [12. friendly], **the most helpful** [13. helpful] people in this country. They're the real reason why I ♥ NY.

Maria Sanchez
New York, New York

3.   **Complete the conversation and say it with a partner.**

FIRST FRIEND: Was that ....you were just

talking to ?

SECOND FRIEND: Uh-huh.

FIRST FRIEND: What .... say? Has she decided

where ....?

SECOND FRIEND: ...., but she says

.... someplace where

....

FIRST FRIEND: Mmm. Why don't you tell .... about

....? From what I've heard,

....

SECOND FRIEND: Really? I've never heard of it. Where

....?

FIRST FRIEND: ....

SECOND FRIEND: OK. I'll tell her about it.

FIRST FRIEND: What else ....?

Did she tell you ....?

SECOND FRIEND: ....

UNIT 2 Happy birthday!

1. WRITING SKILLS. Mac's friend Tom doesn't have a phone, so Maria went over to his house to invite him to the party. He wasn't home, so she left this note under his door. Put in the missing punctuation and capital letters.

[Handwritten note with markings:]

— contraction — apostrophe

tom

Im having a surprise birthday party for Mac this Saturday can you come everybody's meeting at Mac's neighbor's apartment (688 Columbus ave apt 3G) at 7:45 please give me a call to let me know if you're coming my number is 886-9785 Im usually home after 10:00

Maria

[On cake: HAPPY BIRTHDAY MAC]

Was Mac surprised?
Why doesn't Maria borrow Mac's camera?

At eight o'clock Maria and Paula and all the guests went down the hall to Mac's door. Everybody was giggling and whispering, as Maria rang the doorbell. Mac unlocked the door and opened it.

"Surprise! Happy birthday!"

Everybody started singing.

"Happy birthday to you.
Happy birthday to you.
Happy birthday, dear Ma-ac.
Happy birthday to you."

Mac laughed and thanked everybody as they crowded into his apartment carrying food, drinks and other things for the party. He wiped the shaving cream off his face and kissed Maria.

"Happy birthday," she said.

"Thanks, honey. This is a wonderful surprise."

"Were you really surprised?"

"Don't I look it?"

"Yeah, you do. I wish I had my camera so I could take your picture."

"Like *this?* Give me a break."

"Oh, come on. It'd be fun to have some pictures."

"Well, I've got one you can use. I'll get it for you. Just let me finish getting dressed first. Oh, wait a minute, I don't have any film. But I think Paula has a camera. Why don't you ask her if you can use it?"

"OK. Go get dressed."

HAPPY BIRTHDAY TO YOU by Mildred J. Hill and Patty S. Hill, Copyright © 1935 by Summy-Birchard Music. Used by Permission.

2. CONVERSATION. Offer to lend something or suggest someone else who might be able to lend something.

A: I wish I had .... so *I/we* could ....
B: I've got *one/some* you can use. I'll get *it/them* for you.   OR   I think .... has *one/some*. Why don't you ask .... if you can use *it/ them?*
A: OK. Thanks.

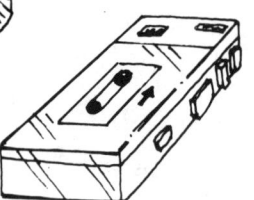

3. WRITING SKILLS. Write a short, informal note inviting someone to a party. Be sure to include all the necessary information. Use Maria's note to Tom on page 13 as a model.

Why does Mac want a roommate?
What's Larry Allen like?

Mac finished getting dressed and then went into the kitchen to fix himself a drink. Two friends of his were there, Tom Sturmond and Bob Vitali.

TOM: Nice party, Mac.

BOB: Yeah. And I like your apartment too. It must be nice to live in a big place like this.

MAC: Yeah, but it's expensive for one person. Actually, I've been thinking about getting a roommate. Do you guys know anybody who's looking for a place to live?

TOM: As a matter of fact, I do. One of the guys in my physics class is looking for a place.

MAC: Oh, yeah? Anybody I know?

TOM: I think so. Larry Allen? He was in our statistics class last spring. Tall, skinny guy? Big nose?

MAC: No, I don't remember him.

BOB: You don't mean that guy who always sits in the back row and sleeps?

MAC: Come on, you guys. Be serious.

TOM: No, really, he's OK. He's just a little ... slow.

MAC: Great! Just what I need. Oh, well, ... do you have his phone number? I'll give him a call.

TOM: No, but I can get it for you Monday.

MAC: OK.

4.   CONVERSATION

> **A:**   You're looking for one of these things:
> - an apartment to share
> - a roommate
> - a part-time job
>
> Ask **B** if he/she knows anybody who might help you.

> **B:**   You know somebody who might help **A**.
> Tell **A** about the person and describe him or her.

A: Do you know anybody who's looking for *a place to live/a roommate/a part-time* _(name of job)_ ?

B: As a matter of fact, I do. One of .... is looking for *a place/one*.

A: Oh, yeah? Anybody I know?*

B: I think so. _(the person's name)_ ? *He/She* was _(information about the person)_ . _(description of the person)_ ?

A: No, I don't remember *him/her*.   OR   Oh, yeah. I know who you mean.

* Note: The full form is *Is it anybody I know?*

> *GRAMMAR NOTE:*
>
> ... one of ⎰ my neighbors ...
>   ⎨ the guys in my class ...
>   ⎱ the people I work with ...

Here are some words you can use to describe people. Most of the words are positive or neutral, but sometimes the words marked with an asterisk(*) are uncomplimentary.

little	big	young
short	tall	older (old *)
thin (skinny *)	heavy (fat *)	beautiful
		good-looking
		cute
		interesting-looking
		(weird-looking *)

with ⎰ glasses
     ⎪ a mustache
     ⎪ a beard
     ⎨ long
     ⎪ short
     ⎪ red   ⎱ hair
     ⎪ straight
     ⎱ curly

What's the matter with Maria?
Whose glasses did Maria find?

Mac left Tom and Bob in the kitchen and went out to the living room to find Maria. She was sitting on the couch with Paula. She smiled at Mac from across the room and he went over to talk to them.

"Mac, have you got any aspirin?" asked Paula.

"What's the matter? Don't you feel well?"

"No. They're for Maria."

Mac looked concerned and sat down next to Maria. "What's the matter?" he asked her.

"Oh, I've got a sore throat and I ache all over. I must be getting a cold or something."

"Oh, no! When did it start?"

"This afternoon at work."

Mac put his arm around her. "You mean, you were sick and you did all this? Listen, why don't you take some Coldstop? I've got some in the bathroom."

"OK. Maybe that'll help."

"That's what I took the last time I had a cold," said Paula. "It worked pretty well."

"Stay right here," Mac said to Maria. "I'll get it for you."

"Thanks," she said. "Oh, by the way, does either of you know whose glasses these are? They were on the couch and I almost sat on them."

"They might be George's," said Paula. "He was sitting here before."

"No, they don't look like his," said Mac. "They must be Bob's. He has a pair like that."

5. CONVERSATION. Say you don't feel well. Suggest something to make someone feel better.

A: What's the matter? Don't you feel well?
B: No. .... I/It must be ....
A: Why don't you ....?
B: OK. Maybe that'll help.

Here are some symptoms.

I've got
- a headache.
- a stomachache.
- a sore throat.
- a runny nose.
- an upset stomach.
- a bad cough.
- a fever.
- chills. — cold

I ache all over.

I can't
- eat.
- sleep.
- breathe.
- stop coughing.
- stop sneezing.
- stop shivering.

My nose is congested/ stuffed up.

Here are some ways to generalize about how you feel:

I must be getting a cold/ the flu.
It must be something I ate.

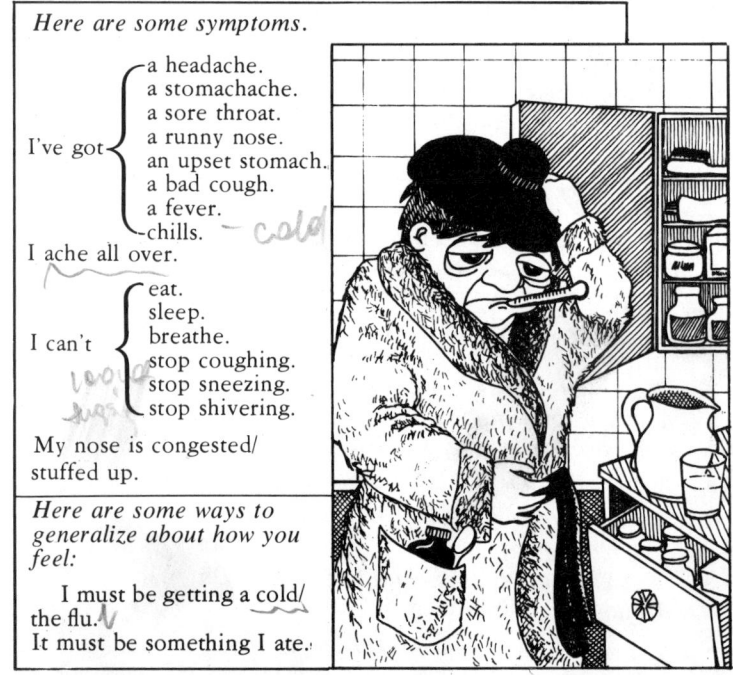

6. LISTENING. You will hear a television commercial for Coldstop, the medicine that Mac recommended to Maria. Listen and check (✔) the things the pharmacist says about Coldstop.

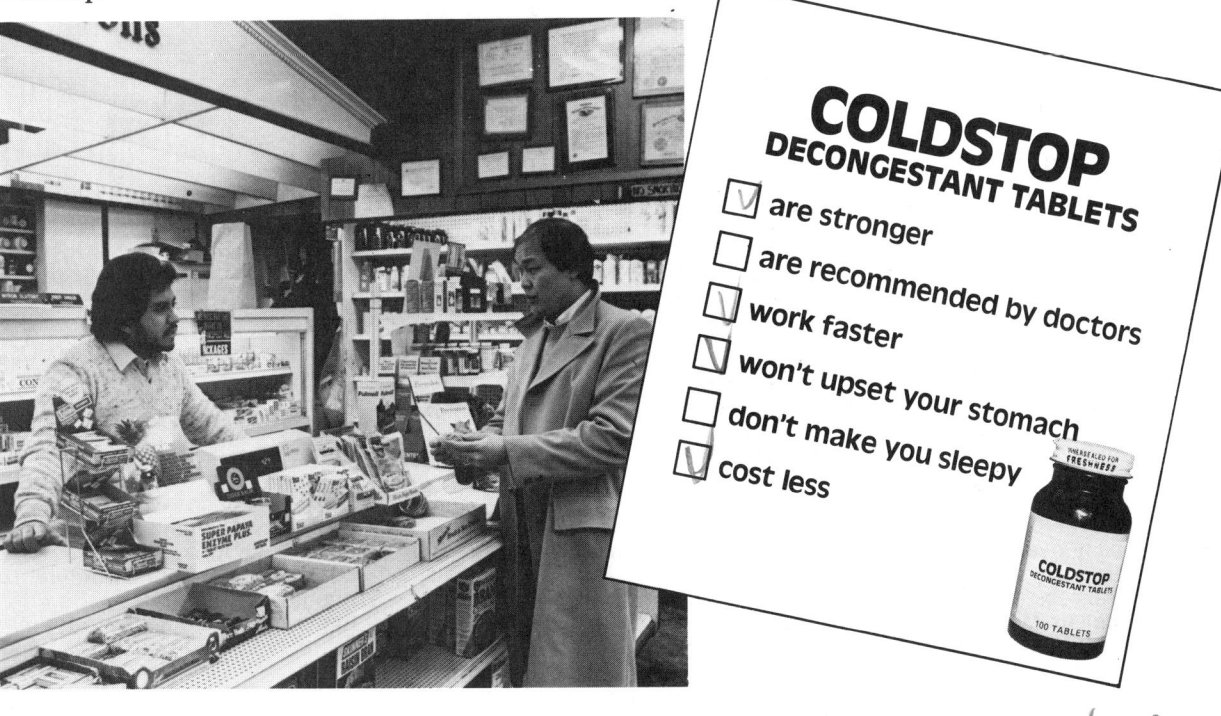

COLDSTOP
DECONGESTANT TABLETS

- ☑ are stronger
- ☐ are recommended by doctors
- ☑ work faster
- ☑ won't upset your stomach
- ☐ don't make you sleepy
- ☑ cost less

7. CONVERSATION. You've found something. Ask who it belongs to.

A: Do you know whose .... *this is/these are?*
B: .... *might/must* be ....'s *(Say why you think so.)* OR   I don't know. Why don't you ask ....?

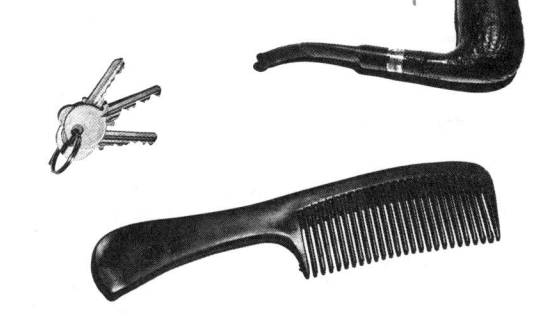

8. FORM. Complete the conversation and say it with a partner. Use the information in parentheses.

MAC: Do you know whose ....
          1. (Mac wants to know
.... ?
who the lighter belongs to.)

MARIA: Uh-uh. Where'd you find it?

MAC: On the table by the sofa.

MARIA: I don't know, but ....
                2. (Maria thinks it might
....
be Tom's because he was sitting there.)
He ....

MAC: No. It's got the initials *PJD* on it. It can't be Tom's.

MAGGIE: Oh, ...
                        3.(Maggie says it must be Paula's.)

MAC: What does the *J* stand for?

MAGGIE: Jane. She hates it.

THE ORDINARY PEPPLES OF ST. LOUIS, MISSOURI, ARE JUST LIKE YOU AND ME—BUT MORE SO

The Average American

. . . **goofs off 45 minutes each workday.**

Republished from Garry Clifford, PEOPLE Weekly, March 16, 1981. © 1981, 1ume inc.

He is a white male, about 30
years old, 5′9″, 172 pounds. She,
5 also white, is a bit younger, stands
5′4½″ and weighs 143 pounds. They
have one child. Together, they earn
$20,268 annually and are $14,000 in
debt. Separately, they drink 374
10 beers, eat 92 hot dogs and swallow
215 aspirins every year. They are
the Statistically Average American
Family, and in a current book called
American Averages (Dolphin,
15 $7.95), journalists Mike Feinsilber
and William Mead have compiled
almost every imaginable detail
about them except one: Do they
really exist? The authors doubt it.
20 "Although average describes all of
us," they write, "it describes none
of us."

. . . **uses 60 gallons of water
a day.**

---

25 It may not, but without too
much effort, *People* magazine was
able to find one family that comes
awfully close to matching the
national norm. They are the
30 Pepples: Kim, 32, Colleen, 31, and
their daughter, Kelly, almost 1½.
The Pepples live in St. Louis
and, like most Americans, own their
home (in this case, a $40,000
35 residence they have converted into
four apartments). Kim, who is just
an inch shorter than the average
man, runs his own public relations
business in suburban Webster
40 Groves. Colleen, an inch taller than
the average woman—and right at

. . . **goes to the library twice a
year . . . to movies five times a
year.**

---

45 the mean weight for her age—holds
a job, like most American women.
She is a part-time personnel
assistant in a local hospital. The
Pepples' combined salary is
50 approximately the national average
for a two-income household,
although their total debt is a bit
lower—about $10,000. The Pepples
own six radios and two television
55 sets, which is average; and they
wash eight loads of clothes a week,
which also matches the national
norm. Like most Americans, who
consume 94.5 pounds of beef
60 annually, the Pepples eat a lot of
hamburger, as often as four times a
week. "I fix it various ways," says

. . . **will move 14 times in his or
her life.**

---

65 Colleen, "from spaghetti to
casseroles." Colleen also does
most of the housework, which is
typical. Objects Kim: "I take the
garbage out twice a week." Also
70 typical.

. . . **eats faster than his or her
parents and grandparents . . .
drinks more alcohol than the
average citizen of any country
75 except Russia and Poland.**

Like most Americans, the Pepples are feeling the pinch of the slumping economy. Faced with mounting debts, they recently
80 locked their charge cards in a safe-deposit box. Like most couples, the Pepples' worst arguments are about money. "That's all we argue about," says
85 Kim. "It becomes serious at times. Colleen is hard-headed. I don't want to owe anybody anything. After we got married (three years ago), we owed everybody. Locking
90 the cards up was the only solution."

. . . will eat 150 steers, 9,000 chickens, 225 lambs, 26 sheep, 310 hogs and 26 acres of grains by age 70.

---

95   Money problems aside, the Pepples share a typical American dream: They spend nearly every weekend looking for a house in the western St. Louis suburb of
100 Webster Groves, where Kim grew up, the son of a banker. Colleen, who is the daughter of a sales executive, wants a three-bedroom

---

**. . . produces, in the course of a
105 lifetime, a pile of garbage equal to 600 to 700 times his or her weight.**

---

home with a backyard and a dog. Even though that dream is
110 deferred, the couple claim that "Life is satisfying." That too is just about par; 90 percent of Americans find their lives agreeable. "Initially, it was ego-deflating to think of
115 myself as average," says Kim. "I like to think I'm different. I own my own business, work harder than most men and am my own boss. Since looking at the statistics and finding
120 that I am average, though, I've learned to get comfortable with it."

—GARRY CLIFFORD

. . . laughs 15 times a day.

---

9. READING STRATEGY: Using the dictionary. Circle the number of the definition that is closest to the meaning of the word in the article.

1. lines 9, 52, 79
   debt n **1** something that someone owes someone else, such as money or services **2** a morally wrong action; a sin.

2. line 7
   earn v **1** to receive something (salary, wages, etc.) for your work **2** to deserve: *He earned that traffic ticket.*

3. line 79
   mount v **1** to climb: *They mounted the stairs.* **2** to get on an animal or a vehicle: *She mounted the horse.* **3** to increase: *Our problems have steadily mounted this week.*

4. lines 87, 89
   owe v **1** to have to pay; to be in debt: *I still owe $3,000 on my car.* **2** to have a moral debt: *I owe you my thanks.*

5. line 77
   pinch n **1** the action of squeezing between the thumb and finger **2** the quantity that can be picked up with thumb and forefinger: *a pinch of salt* **3** difficulty caused by not having necessary resources such as money, time or materials.

6. line 78
   slump v, n **1** to fall suddenly: *He slumped into a chair.* **2** a sudden decrease as in income, business, production.

10. READING STRATEGY: Getting the meaning from context. Do these expressions from the article mean *average, almost average* or *not average?* Circle the answer.

1. *Ordinary* (title) means
   a. average.
   b. almost average.
   c. not average.

2. *Just like you and me* (title) means
   a. average.
   b. almost average.
   c. not average.

3. *Close to matching the national norm* (lines 28–29) means
   a. average.
   b. almost average.
   c. not average.

4. *An inch taller than the average woman* (lines 40–41) means
   a. average.
   b. almost average.
   c. not average.

5. *Right at the mean weight* (lines 41, 45) means

a. average.
b. almost average.
c. not average.

6. *Matches the national norm* (lines 57–58) means
   a. average.
   b. almost average.
   c. not average.

7. *Typical* (lines 68, 70) means
   a. average.
   b. almost average.
   c. not average.

8. *Just about par* (lines 111–112) means
   a. average.
   b. almost average.
   c. not average.

9. *Different* (line 116) means
   a. average.
   b. almost average.
   c. not average.

11. READING STRATEGIES: Inferring and finding specific information. Circle *true* or *false*. Then indicate how you arrived at your answers.

1. The average American family has two children. True or false?
   The information you needed was (circle one)
   a. stated in the article.
   b. implied but not stated.

2. Most American women have jobs. True or false?
   The information you needed was
   a. stated in the article.
   b. implied but not stated.

3. Kim and Colleen make about $20,000 a year. True or false?
   The information you needed was
   a. stated in the article.
   b. implied but not stated.

4. Most American couples share the housework equally. True or false?
   The information you needed was
   a. stated in the article.
   b. implied but not stated.

5. Houses in Webster Groves are more expensive than the Pepples' house in St. Louis. True or false?
   The information you needed was
   a. stated in the article.
   b. implied but not stated.

6. The Pepples don't have a very happy marriage. True or false?
   The information you needed was
   a. stated in the article.
   b. implied but not stated.

REVIEW

YOU'VE LEARNED TO

talk about something that you don't have:	I wish I had my camera so I could take your picture.
offer to lend something:	I've got a camera you can use. I'll get it for you.
make a suggestion:	I think Paula has a camera. Why don't you ask her if you can use it?
ask for information:	Do you know anybody who's looking for a place to live?
identify and describe people:	Larry Allen? He was in our statistics class last spring. Tall, skinny guy? Big nose?
talk about sickness:	What's the matter? Don't you feel well? No, I've got a sore throat and I ache all over. I must be getting a cold or something.
ask who something belongs to:	Do you know whose glasses these are?
talk about probability:	They might be George's. He was sitting here before.
state a conclusion:	They must be Bob's. He has a pair like that.

GRAMMAR

Wish + Past Tense

I **wish I had** my camera.

So (that) + Clause (Purpose)

I wish I had my camera **so** (that) I could take your picture.

Ellipsis

Anybody I know? = **Is it** anybody I know?

Relative Clause: Who

Do you know anybody **who's looking for a place to live?**

Whose in Embedded Questions

Do you know { **whose** glasses **these are?** / **whose** lighter **this is?** }

Might/Must

They **might** be George's. He was sitting here.
They **must** be Bob's. He has a pair like that.
I **must** be getting a cold. I've got a sore throat.

One/It/Some/Them

I've got **one** you can use. I'll get **it** for you.

I've got **some** you can use. I'll get **them** for you.

ask . . . if

Why don't you **ask** her **if** you can use it?

USEFUL WORDS AND EXPRESSIONS

ache	cold	congested	straight
ate (eat)	cough	curly	stuffed up
breathe	fever	cute	tall
cough	flu	fat	thin
mean	guy	good-looking	weird-looking
shiver	headache	heavy	young
sleep	initial	interesting-looking	•
sneeze	mustache	long	whose
stand for	nose	old	•
use	roommate	older	all over
've (have) got	stomach	runny	I think so.
•	stomachache	short	too bad
beard	throat	skinny	What's the matter?
chills	•	sore	

1.   ROLE PLAY

A: You need a roommate. Ask **B** if he/she knows anyone who's looking for a place to live. If **B** knows somebody, ask about the person.

B: You know somebody who wants to share a house or an apartment. Tell **A** about the person.

2.   Two high school students are talking. Complete the conversation and say it with a partner.

3.   Some friends are having a picnic. One of them forgot to bring a radio. Complete the conversation and say it with a partner.

FIRST FRIEND: I wish I had ....
    so ....

SECOND FRIEND: I think Diane .... Why
    don't you ask her if ....?

FIRST FRIEND: She just told me she's going home. She doesn't feel well.

SECOND FRIEND: .... matter?

FIRST FRIEND: ....

SECOND FRIEND: It must be those four hamburgers she ate.

4. Maria was sick and couldn't go to work on Monday. She called her doctor, but he wasn't in so she left a message. Later, the doctor called her back. Complete the conversation and do the puzzle.

DR. MARSH: Hello, Ms. Sanchez. This is Dr. Marsh. Sorry I took so long.

MARIA: Dr. Marsh, I'm glad you called. I feel .... (4. down)

DR. MARSH: What's the ....? (6. across)

MARIA: I've got a ...., a .... (1. across) (6. down) .... and a .... (7. down) (3. down) (3. across) and I can't .... (2. across)

DR. MARSH: It sounds like the .... Do you (4. across) have a .... or ....? (1. down) (5. across)

MARIA: Yeah, my temperature's 101° and I can't stop .... I .... all over and (5. down) (2. down) I've got an .... (8. down) (9. across)

DR. MARSH: Are you ....? (7. across)

MARIA: Yeah. Sometimes I can't stop.

DR. MARSH: All right. I'll telephone the drugstore with a prescription for your .... Do (8. across) you want me to ask them to deliver it?

MARIA: Yes, thank you, and thanks for calling.

DR. MARSH: Don't mention it. Drink plenty of liquids and try to sleep. If you don't feel better in the morning, call me.

MARIA: OK. Thank you.

DR. MARSH: Goodbye.

UNIT 3 Have you ever considered a career in sales?

WHAT KIND OF WORK WOULD YOU ENJOY MOST?

As people grow and change, their interests change too—sometimes so much that they no longer enjoy their present hobbies, leisure activities, or even their work. Many people don't notice these changes in themselves and they often don't understand why they have become bored or unmotivated at work.

Whether you are still in school or already have a job, it might be interesting to talk to a career counselor or take a vocational test to help you match your interests and abilities to a specific job or career area. If that isn't possible, you should at least discuss your interests with your family and friends. They know you and they can often help. The questionnaire below can also help you decide what kind of work is best for you.

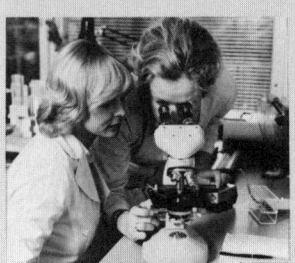
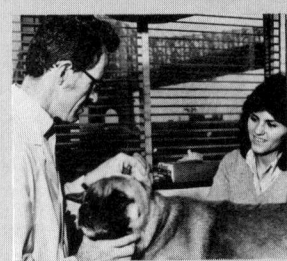

Answer the three questions below. Indicate only what you really *enjoy*—not what you know.

A. Which of these are you most interested in? (Check one or two.)
   1. .... numbers, symbols, logic
   2. .... words, ideas, languages
   3. .... colors, forms
   4. .... music
   5. .... body movement (dance, athletics)
   6. .... tools and materials
   7. .... animals, plants
   8. .... other (specify)
   ....

B. What kind of work do you prefer? (Check one in each set.)
   1a. .... physically active work
    b. .... physically inactive work

   2a. .... work done alone
    b. .... work done with others

   3a. .... routine work
    b. .... creative work

   4a. .... work done indoors
    b. .... work done outdoors

   5a. .... work done for yourself
    b. .... work done for someone else

C. Show your questionnaire to your family and friends and discuss it with them. See what kind of work they think you would enjoy. After that, it's up to you!

Why does Ms. Poole suggest another field to Mac?
Why does she suggest sales specifically?
What does Mac think of her suggestion?

"I'm sorry, Mr. MacDonald, but I don't think we'll be able to offer you a position at this time."

Mac was shocked. This was his third interview and every time he'd gotten the same response. He decided to find out what the problem was. "Could you tell me why not?"

"Well, basically, it's because your grades aren't high enough. We require at least a B+ average."

"I see. . . . You know, Ms. Poole, I've heard a lot about Carey Industries and I was really hoping to work there. What if I do well on my final exams? Do you think I could schedule another interview?"

"I really couldn't say. You see, we'll probably fill all our openings before the end of May . . . but it might be worth a try."

"All right. Thank you."

Mac was ready to leave, but Ms. Poole picked up his resume and studied it for a moment. "I see that you worked for the Parks and Recreation Council in Chicago for several summers. What did you do there?"

"My job was to go around to clubs and neighborhood groups and tell people about the sports and cultural programs that were available so they could take advantage of them."

"How did you like that?"

"I liked it a lot. I met all kinds of people and got to see parts of the city I'd never been to before."

The recruiter nodded. "Mr. MacDonald, have you ever considered a career in sales? Most of the large engineering firms have sales divisions, you know, and your engineering background could be an advantage."

"No, I've never really thought about it. That's an interesting idea. I think I'd rather stay in engineering, though."

"Well, you do seem to have the personality for sales. Why don't you think about it?"

"Thank you. I will."

"Well, Mr. MacDonald," said the recruiter, standing up, "thank you for your interest in Carey Industries and good luck."

"Thank you, Ms. Poole. You've been very helpful."

1.   FORMAL AND INFORMAL LANGUAGE. Match each item on the left with the one on the right that means about the same. One pair is matched as an example.

FORMAL	INFORMAL
• I don't think we'll be able to offer you a position at this time.	• Did you ever think about sales?
• Could you tell me why not?	• I don't know.
• I really couldn't say.	• OK. Thanks.
• Have you ever considered a career in sales?	• We can't give you a job right now.
• All right. Thank you.	• How come?

2.   CONVERSATION. Explain why you can't give someone a job, a promotion or a passing grade.

A: I'm sorry, *(name)*, but I don't think *I'll/we'll* be able to ....

B: Could you tell me why not?

A: Well, basically, it's because *(of)* ....

B: What if ....? Do you think ....?

A: I really couldn't say, but it might be worth a try.

B: All right. Thank you.

A *can explain like this:*   chase

It's because { you don't have enough experience.
you haven't turned in all your assignments.
you don't meet all the requirements.
your work hasn't been satisfactory.

It's because of { your grades.
your attendance record.   noun phrase

B *can respond like this:*

What if { I come back when I have some experience?
I do well on my final exams?
I improve my attendance?
I work harder?

3.   CONVERSATION. Look at the questionnaire that your partner filled out on page 23. Talk about your partner's preferences, and suggest occupations like this:

A: I see *you're interested in/you like* <u>*(item from*</u>
<u>*questionnaire)*</u>. Have you ever considered <u>*(career*</u>

<u>*area)*</u>*/becoming a* <u>*(job title)*</u> ?

B: No, I've never really thought about it. That's an interesting idea, though. OR   That's an interesting idea. I think I'd rather ...., though.

A: Well, why don't you think about it? <u>*(another*</u>
<u>*reason for your suggestion)*</u> .

B: Thank you. I will.

Career Areas	
accounting	medicine
architecture	movies
banking	nursing
biology	politics
business	psychology
chemistry	religion
computers	sales
construction	sports
ecology	television
engineering	theater
journalism	writing

Job Titles	
artist	lawyer
computer programer	musician
dancer	pilot
dentist	reporter
electrician	secretary
fashion designer	singer
fashion model	social worker
flight attendant	teacher
illustrator	tourist guide
interpreter/translator	veterinarian

4.   ▭ LISTENING. After his interview, Mac ran into his friend Tom. Listen to their conversation and answer the questions.

1.   Tom wants to talk about
    a.   his career plans.
    b.   Mac's career plans.

2.   Who wants to change the subject of the conversation?
    a.   Mac.
    b.   Tom.

3.   Does he succeed in changing it?
    a.   Yes.
    b.   No.

How does Mac feel about the interview?
What does Maria say to encourage him?
Why doesn't Maria go with Paula?

Mac was depressed after the interview. A little while after he got home, Maria came over to his apartment. As soon as she saw him, she knew the interview hadn't gone well.

"I got turned down again," he said.

"Oh, no!"

"They said it was because of my grades. I wish I'd studied harder these last few months."

Maria followed Mac into the living room and sat down next to him. "But you *have* studied hard. Don't let it get you down, Mac. You'll get a job. Just be patient."

Mac nodded. "I guess you're right, but in the meantime, I've got to do well on my exams. I'm not going to be able to go out much."

"That's OK. I've got exams soon too. We can study together."

Mac wasn't sure how much studying he'd do with Maria there, but he agreed. "OK, it's a deal."

"OK," said Maria. "You get to work and I'll go make some coffee."

A little while later the doorbell rang and Maria went to answer it. It was Paula.

"Oh, hi, Maria. Hi, Mac. Are you two doing any-thing this evening? I was thinking of going to see *All That Jazz* and I don't feel like going alone."

"Thanks, but I have to study," said Mac regretfully.

Maria knew Mac was depressed and she wanted to stay with him. "I'd really like to go with you," she said, "but I have to study too. How about tomorrow?"

"No, I'm seeing Ray tomorrow night, but maybe we can go some other time."

5. CONVERSATION

A: You just got fired, thrown out of school or turned down for a job/raise/promotion. Tell B what happened.	B: A is upset and discouraged. Try to make him/her feel better.

A: I just got ....

B: Oh, no!

A: .... said it was because (*of*) .... I wish *I'd/I hadn't* ....

B: Don't let it get you down. ....

A: Yeah, I guess you're right.

A *can express regret like this:*	B *can encourage like this:*
I wish I'd { worked harder. / gone to class more often. / taken the job more seriously. I wish I hadn't { wasted so much time. / been absent so often. / been so sure I'd get it.	You'll get another job. They'll let you back in school soon. You'll get one sooner or later.

6. GRAMMAR FOCUS. Mac read this article in a student newspaper. Fill in the blanks with the correct words.

HOW TO AVOID THOSE POST-INTERVIEW BLUES

After being interviewed for a job, many people find themselves thinking "I wish I _hadn't been_ so nervous"
                         1. haven't been/hadn't been
or "I wish I _answered_ that question better."
            2. 've answered/'d answered
Has it ever happened to you? If you've _already had_
3. Has/Had   4. already have/
already had one or several "bad" interviews,
already had

7.   READING STRATEGY: Predicting.

The rest of the article in Exercise 6 probably:
    a. tells something funny that happened to the writer during a job interview.
    (b.) gives advice to people who are going to have job interviews.
    c. tells employers how they should interview people.

Explain the reasons for your answer.

8.   CONVERSATION. Invite someone to do something.   Then agree on a time.

A: Are you doing anything _(time)_ ? I was
     thinking of _____-ing _____.
B: I'd really like to go with you, but _____.
     How about _____?
A: _(Agree or say why you can't)._
B: Good. That'll be fun.   OR   Well, maybe
     we can go some other time.

Going Out
a weekly
magazine

April 26, 1980   Vol. 7

Contents

9.   **WRITING SKILLS.** You are going to write a letter applying for a job. First read the want ad and the notes and letter below.

April 28, 1980

New York News

WAITERS/WAITRESSES
Restaurant in large midtown hotel needs exp'd waiters/ waitresses for bfst/lnch/dnr. Good personality. Other language helpful. Gd tips, bnfts. Call: (212) 841-4000. Write: Box K8962, NY News, 99 W. 38 St., NYC 10018

This is an ad that Maria placed in the *New York News* while she was working in the Personnel Department at the Regency.

The ad was answered by Christine Estes of Philadelphia, Pennsylvania. These are the notes that Ms. Estes used to plan her letter of application.

> Waitress part time mornings
> N.Y. News Apr. 28
> *experience* — 6 mos. counter
> Al's All Nite Cafe
> 10 mos. (to present) lunch,
> dinner Luau — family-
> style Polynesian
> some Spanish
> *personality* — pleasant,
> reliable, efficient
> *availability* — 2 wks.
> notice to Luau

This is the letter that Ms. Estes sent in answer to the ad.

> *sender's address*
>
> 3798 Woodland Ave., Apt. B
> Philadelphia, Pennsylvania 19104
> April 29, 1980
>
> *{ 2 blank lines*
> *{ inside address*
>
> Box K8962
> New York News
> 99 West 38th Street
> New York, New York 10018
>
> *{ one blank line*
>
> Dear Sir or Madam: *{ one colon*
> *{ one blank line*
>
> I would like to apply for the waitress position which you advertised in the New York News on April 28. I would like to work part time, preferably in the mornings.
>
> I worked for six months as a counter waitress in a diner. For the last ten months I have served lunch and dinner at the Luau, a family-style Polynesian restaurant here in Philadelphia. I also speak some Spanish.
>
> My supervisors consider me pleasant, reliable and efficient. I think I would do a good job for you.
>
> I am available immediately, except that I will need to give my present employer two weeks' notice. You can reach me at the address above or at (215) 873-5411.
>
> Sincerely,
>
> *Christine Estes*
>
> Christine Estes
>
> encl.

Now, look at these "help wanted" ads and find a job you'd like to apply for. Plan your letter the way Ms. Estes planned hers. Then write a letter of application.

Help Wanted

AIRLINE
AIRLINE RESERVATIONS TRAINEES
No airline exp nec but must have exp in contact with public. Opportunity for advancement. Work in NY area or Southeast U.S. Pref bright, responsible bilingual. Good salary, benefits. Free travel on our routes, discounts on other airlines. Helen Davidson, Personnel Director, Transcontinental Airways, 17 E 41 St, NYC 10016. (212) 862-1998

TRAVEL
COLLEGE BKGD
Be a guide/counselor for small groups (10–15) of teens in Europe, Middle East, Far East, Latin America, or Africa this summer. Previous residence or extended travel in area req'd plus fluency in at least one area language. 22–35 yrs. All travel, meals, hotels paid. Reply: GH899 NEWS 78111

INSTRUCTOR
Exclusive women's exercise studio seeks intelligent, attractive instructor for part-time position. Pref dance or athletic bkgd. Will train if nec. Competitive sal. Manhattan Health Spa, 202 E 41 St. 288-8663.

Help Wanted

PHOTOGRAPHER
Summer only. Full/part-time. We will train advanced amateur to photograph children in local day camps. Use our equipment, except must have car and be willing to travel overnight 6–7 days a mo. Mr. Abel, Hunter Studios, 45 W 34 St, NYC 10018. 733-6831

RECEPT $10,000+
MANAGEMENT TRAINEE
Be our receptionist. Test & screen applicants for clerical positions. After 6 mos be eligible for promotion to personnel interviewer at top salary. Applicants must have pleasant personality & good phone voice. GH791 NEWS 78111

RESTAURANT
SEE THE WORLD
As summer days get longer, the ocean breeze is calling. As a cook, waiter or busboy on one of our luxury ocean-liners, you can work and travel at the same time. Ex sal, meals, accommodations. Exp req'd. CANUTE LINE, 619 W 42 St. NYC 10036 or call (212) 737-8287

Help Wanted

SALES $$
SALES REPRESENTATIVE
LATIN AMERICA, AFRICA, SOUTHEAST ASIA. NY-based firm expanding its foreign operations needs sales reps for proven product line. College graduates. English plus Spanish, French or Portuguese a must. First-hand knowledge of area can substitute for sales experience. Will train successful candidates. For app't in your area, write: AF639 NEWS 78111

SEC'Y $13-15,000
DISCO FEVER
VP & Program Director at this popular midtown rock station seeks dedicated right hand who loves the music business to assist him in all phases. Opportunity to meet disc jockeys, top performers & many other interesting people involved in this terrific industry. Ex benefits include 100% medical, dental & free concert tickets. Typing & sten. Personnel Director, WREX, 852 Tenth Ave, NYC 10019. 455-5333

10.   **READING STRATEGY: Getting the meaning from context. Find the abbreviations in the want ads and then write the complete word. The first one is an example.**

EXAMPLE: Find an abbreviation in the eighth ad that means "a person who types letters, files papers and answers the phone for someone": *sec'y* Complete word: *secretary*

1.   Find an abbreviation in the first ad that means "work you did before": .... Complete word: ....
2.   Find an abbreviation in the first and third ads that means about the same as "we want": .... Complete word ....
3.   Find an abbreviation in the third ad that means "experience or studies in this area": .... Complete word: ....
4.   Find an abbreviation in the sixth and eighth ads that means "especially good" or "very high": .... Complete word: ....

11. READING STRATEGY: Finding specific information.
Here is information about three people who have
registered with an employment agency.
Which of the advertised jobs
would you recommend
to each of them?

Michael Voranski, 19
440 E. 26 St, NYC 10010
(212) 481-4310

Personal: Single. Busy social life. Lives in university housing.

Employment goal: A part-time job to help support himself until he finishes college.

Educational background: Physical education major at Hunter College. Graduated from high school last year. Has three more years before he finishes college.

Employment history: Part-time jobs during high school. Worked two summers as a waiter and three summers as a cook. Didn't like the jobs, but the money was good.

Other: Types 45 words per minute. Studied Spanish for three years. Won medals for gymnastics in high school and college. Likes to travel, but hasn't had time or money to travel very much.

Kevin Black, 20
68 Van Reypen St.
Jersey City, N.J. 07306
(201) 963-1178

Personal: Married. Six-month-old daughter. Wife quit job before baby was born. Now makes $8,000 and is using savings to pay monthly bills. Lives in an apartment near his and wife's parents. Doesn't want to move.

Employment goal: A much higher salary.

Educational background: Graduated from high school almost two years ago.

Employment history: Two summers (during high school) worked as a counselor in a Boy Scout camp. Liked working with kids. From high school graduation to present has been a salesman in a department store. Likes working with public, but doesn't like selling.

Other: One year of French in high school, but has forgotten most of it. Interested in sports. Was on basketball and baseball teams in high school.

Penny Atkinson, 24
24 Minetta Lane
NYC 10012
(212) 674-7811

Personal: Single. Shares apartment with a friend.

Employment goal: A more permanent job with possibility of advancement and opportunity to travel.

Educational background: Dropped out of college in her second year to travel. Plans to return to college part time in the fall.

Employment history: Has been a radio announcer, sales clerk, house painter, baby sitter, life guard, taxi driver. Liked the last two jobs best. Now working as a waitress.

Other: Types, but not well. Traveled in Africa for six months. Lived and worked in Greece for a year. Speaks good French and Greek.

REVIEW

YOU'VE LEARNED TO

apologize and give bad news:	I'm sorry, but I don't think we'll be able to offer you a position.
ask for an explanation:	Could you tell me why not?
ask about a possible solution:	What if I do well on my final exams?
avoid committing yourself:	I really couldn't say, but it might be worth a try. Maybe we can go some other time. That's an interesting idea.
make a suggestion:	Have you ever considered a career in sales?/Why don't you think about it?
reject a suggestion:	That's an interesting idea. I think I'd rather stay in engineering, though.
talk about something that happened recently:	I just got fired.
express regret:	I wish I'd studied harder these last few months.
encourage:	Don't let it get you down. You'll get a job.
invite someone to do something:	Are you doing anything this evening? I was thinking of going to see *All That Jazz*.
reject an invitation:	I'd love to, but I have to study.
suggest an alternative:	How about tomorrow?

GRAMMAR

Future with Be able to

> I don't think we'll **be able to** give you a job.

Because (of)

> It's { **because** of your grades.
because your grades aren't high enough. }

What if

> **What if** I do well on my final exams?

Passive Voice

> I just **got** { **fired.**
thrown out of school.
turned down for a raise. }

Wish + Past Perfect

> I wish { I'd **studied** harder.
I hadn't **wasted** so much time. }

Comparative of Adverbs

> I wish I'd { worked **harder**
gone to class **more often.**
taken the job **more seriously.** }

USEFUL WORDS AND EXPRESSIONS

be able to	•	absent	often
become	assignment	another	seriously
consider	attendance	discouraged	•
get fired	exam	enough	all right
get thrown out	experience	final	be interested in
get turned down	grade	satisfactory	be worth
improve	record	•	Don't let it get you down.
let	requirement	back	sooner or later
taken (take)	try	basically	what if
waste	•	harder	why not

1.   George and one of the men he works with are talking during their lunch break. George has just told Bert about losing a job when he was eighteen. Fill in the blanks with the correct form of the verb (for example, *fire, firing* or *fired*).

GEORGE: That was the only job I ever lost. Did *you* ever get .... ?
                                                                                                                                    1. fire

BERT: No, but I got .... out of high school.
                                              2. throw

GEORGE: Yeah? What for?

BERT: Oh, I don't know. I never liked .... a student.
                                                                                                      3. be

            I just wasn't interested in school. They finally ....
                                                                                                                      4. throw

            me out when I stopped going to classes. . . . I ....
                                                                                                                        5. like

            biology, though.

GEORGE: Did you ever .... about .... a biologist?
                                              6. think   7. be

BERT: Nah. Construction work's good enough for me. I'd rather

            .... outdoors anyway. . . . Oh, sure, sometimes
                        8. be
            I think "What if I'd .... high school and gone to
                                                          9. finish
            college?" I guess things would .... different—but
                                                                                            10. be
            they might not .... better.
                                              11. be

2.   CONVERSATION. Talk about getting fired.

A:

| B looks upset. Ask him/her what the matter is. |

B:

| Tell **A** you just got fired and the reason they gave you. |

| Sympathize. |

| Say you regret (not) having done something:
I wish I'd/I hadn't .... |

| Encourage **B**. Make a suggestion |

| React to **A**'s suggestion. |

3.   Something upsetting just happened to you. Complete your conversation with Paula. Then say it with a partner.

YOU: Guess what. I got ....

.... said it was because

....

PAULA: Oh, no! Do you think you'll be able to ....

....?

YOU: I don't know. I wish ....

PAULA: Mmm. . . . Well, I know you're interested in.............................

.... Have you ever considered

....?

YOU: Yeah. I'd really rather ....,

though.

"I just got kicked out of school."

UNIT 4 I was wondering if we could have lunch sometime.

Does Jack have the magazine Paula needs?
Why does Paula want the magazine?
Why is Marilyn Dixon going to call Paula?

Paula Duran was at work at the *New York News* one morning when another reporter, Jack Andropoulos, walked by.

"Hey, Jack!" she called. "Have you still got that magazine?"

"Which one?" he asked.

"You know—the one you showed me yesterday. The one with the article about women journalists."

"Oh, yeah." Jack nodded. "It's at home."

"Do you mind if I borrow it? I'd like to read it."

"Oh, sure," he said. "I'll bring it tomorrow." Jack started to leave, then snapped his fingers. "That reminds me," he said. "A friend of mine is writing an article about working women. I told her to call you. Her name's Marilyn Dixon."

1. CONVERSATION. Identify something and make a request.

A: Have you got *that/those* ....?
B: Which *one/ones*?
A: You know—the *one(s)* ....
B: Oh, yeah. *It's/They're* .... OR Oh, no, I don't. ....

You can continue like this:

A: Do you mind if I ....?
B: Sure. I'll .... OR Sorry. *I'm using/I need* .... right now (*but* ....).

You can describe something like this:

The one(s) { with the red covers.
            in the folder.
            (that) we were working on yesterday.
The new one(s).

subject before a noun

object
it / and
them

2. GRAMMAR FOCUS. Fill in the blanks with *one, ones, that, those, it, them* or *they*.

PAULA: Hey, Jack. I can't find ....*those*........ cassettes I was listening to on Friday. Have
             you got ....*them*........?
                          2

JACK: Which ....*ones*........
              3

PAULA: The ....*ones*........ of my interview with the Johnson family last week.
              4

JACK: Oh, yeah. I put ....*them*........ back on your desk. Aren't ....*they*........ there?
              5   6

PAULA: No, ...*they*........ aren't. Someone else must have borrowed ....*them*........ By the way, I
              7   8
             found ....*that*........ book you were asking me about—the ....*one*........ about nuclear
              9   10
             energy. I'll bring ....*it*........ tomorrow.
              11

JACK: Oh, thanks. I'd really like to read ....*it*.........
                                              12

3.   READ THE AD. Paula found this ad and ordered a subscription to *News in Review*.
Read the ad and circle the answers.

1. *As many as four* means
   a. more than four magazines.
   b. one, two, three or four magazines.
   c. only one magazine.

2. *Up to 50%* means
   a. exactly 50%.
   b. 50% or more.
   c. 50% or less.

READERS' BONANZA!
Get up to 50% off
on your choice of these outstanding publications

Take a good look at these popular maga-
zines. Then take a look at the prices below.
You may choose as many as four of these
titles at our special introductory rates—up
to 50% off! Write to:
**Discount Magazines, P.O. Box 3027,
Denver, Colorado 56001.**
(Enclose check or money order)

HERE'S WHAT YOU SAVE:

NEWS IN REVIEW—52 ISSUES, ONLY $24.99 (Regular rate $35.00)
                             26 ISSUES, ONLY $14.00 (Regular rate $17.50)
CYCLE MAGAZINE—10 ISSUES, ONLY $4.99 (Regular rate $10.00)
SPORTS REPORT—12 ISSUES, ONLY $7.75 (Regular rate $15.00)
MODERN HOMEMAKER—12 ISSUES, ONLY $10.00 (Regular rate $18.00)
                              6 ISSUES, ONLY $6.00 (Regular rate $9.00)
TEEN DIGEST—12 ISSUES, ONLY $8.50 (Regular rate $14.40)
                     6 ISSUES, ONLY $5.25 (Regular rate $7.20)
STEREO NEWS—16 ISSUES ONLY $6.99 (Regular rate $11.25)
                       12 ISSUES, ONLY $5.25 (Regular rate $8.50)
FASHION—9 ISSUES, ONLY $4.99 (Regular rate $11.25)

STEREO NEWS

News in review

CYCLE

SPORTS REPORT

MODERN HOMEMAKER

TEEN DIGEST

FASHION

4. WRITING SKILLS. Look at the ad again. Decide
which magazine(s) you would like to subscribe to and
write a letter ordering the magazine(s). Use the checklist below to
plan your letter. Which of the items should you include in your letter?

☑ Your address
☑ The date
☑ The address of Discount Magazines
☐ *Dear Discount Magazines,*
☑ Dear Sir or Madam:
☑ The names of the magazines you want to subscribe to
☐ Your reason for choosing each magazine

☑ How many issues you want of each magazine
☐ The regular price of each magazine
☑ The amount of the check or money order you are enclosing
☑ Thank you
☐ Love,
☑ Sincerely,
☑ Your signature

Where are Marilyn and Paula going to meet?
Why did Paula suggest it?

Not long after Jack and Paula had talked, Jack's friend called Paula at work.

PAULA: Paula Duran.

MARILYN: Ms. Duran, my name's Marilyn Dixon. Jack Andropoulos suggested that I call you.

PAULA: Oh, yes. He said you might call. How can I help you?

MARILYN: Well, I'm writing an article about working women and I was wondering if we could have lunch sometime this week. I'd like to talk to you about your job at the *News*.

PAULA: Oh, OK. When would you like to meet?

MARILYN: How about Thursday at one?

PAULA: Let me check my calendar . . . uh . . . sure, that's fine. Where would you like to meet?

MARILYN: Can you suggest a place that's convenient for you?

PAULA: How about the Red Onion on West 39th Street? It's between Fifth and Sixth. It's not too expensive and it's quiet.

MARILYN: Fine. Then I'll see you there on Thursday at one o'clock.

Note the use of the base form after suggest
every after a third person singular subject.
suggested that she call you.

5. CONVERSATION. Identify yourself. Ask for and make an appointment.

A: *(your full name)*.

B: *Mr./Ms./Miss/Mrs.* ...., my name's *(your full name)*. *(a friend's name)* suggested that I call you.

A: Oh, yes. How can I help you?

B: *I'm/I* .... and I was wondering if we could have *lunch/dinner/coffee/a drink* sometime.

A: OK. When would you like to meet?

B: How about ...*(day)*... at ...*(hour)*...?

A: That's fine. Where would you like to meet?

B: Can you suggest a place?

A: How about ...*(place)*... on ...*(street)*... *(between/near/across from)* ....?

B: Fine. Then I'll see you there on ...*(day)*... at ...*(hour)*....

> *You can say:*
>
> I'm writing an article/a report/a paper about working women.
> I'm looking for information about nuclear energy.
> I need some information about the *New York News*.
> I'm interested in journalism.
> I'd like to ask you about your job.

6. 📼 **LISTENING. Read Paula's appointment book. Someone is calling her to change an appointment. Listen to the conversation and make the necessary changes in her book. The change in her first appointment is an example.**

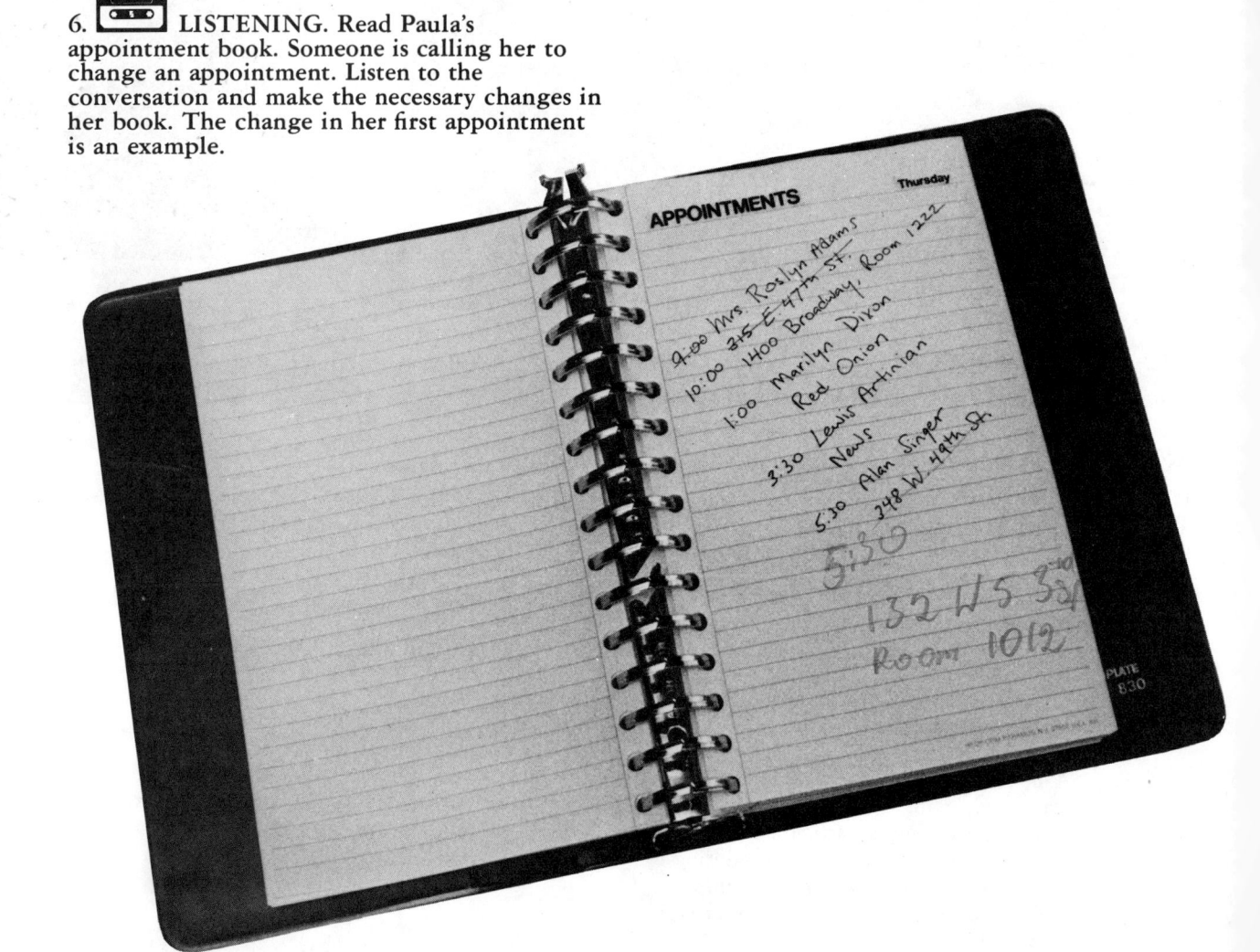

Why does Marilyn say she's sorry?
Do Paula and Marilyn order the same lunch?

On Thursday Paula got to the restaurant before Marilyn Dixon did. After a few minutes a tall young woman arrived. "Excuse me, are you Paula Duran?"

Paula smiled and held out her hand. "Yes," she said. "And you must be Marilyn Dixon."

"I'm sorry I'm late. Have you been waiting long?"

"No, I just got here."

Paula and Marilyn followed the waiter to a table and sat down. He gave them menus and asked if they would like a drink before lunch, but neither of them wanted one. While they were looking at their menus, the waiter brought bread and butter and filled their water glasses. A few minutes later he returned. "Are you ready to order?" he asked.

"Go ahead, Paula," said Marilyn. "I haven't decided yet."

"I'd like roast beef," said Paula, "but no potato, please."

"And how would you like your roast beef?"

"Medium."

"Peas and carrots or spinach?" he asked.

"Spinach."

"Would you like anything to start with?"

"No, thanks."

"Something to drink?" he asked.

"Not right now, thanks," said Paula.

Paula handed him the menu and began to butter a piece of bread. The waiter turned to Marilyn. "And what would you like?"

"I'll have a club sandwich on rye and a green salad. Do you have Russian dressing?"

"I'm sorry, we only have Italian, French and Roquefort."

"OK. Italian. Oh, and could I have another fork? This one's dirty."

"Oh. Sorry. Will there be anything else?"

"Would you please bring us some more butter?" asked Paula.

"Sure."

7. CONVERSATION. Find someone you're supposed to meet.

A: Excuse me, are you ....?

B: Yes. And you must be ....

A: Have you been waiting long?

B: No, I just got here.

the RED ONION

APPETIZERS

Shrimp Cocktail	3.25
Fresh Fruit Cup	1.50

SOUPS

Cream of Tomato	1.25
Vegetable	1.25
French Onion	2.00

SALADS

Green Salad	1.25
mixed greens, with French, Italian or Roquefort dressing	
Red Onion Salad	1.75
lettuce, tomato, mushrooms, bacon with our own Red Onion dressing	

ENTREES

Roast Beef	5.95
served with vegetables and baked potato	
Club Sandwich	4.50
turkey, bacon, lettuce and tomato on rye or white toast served with french fries	
Beef Stew	3.95
beef, carrots, peas and potatoes in our special gravy	
Fried Chicken	4.95
served with vegetables and french fries	
Bluefish	5.50
served with vegetables and baked potato	
Spaghetti and Meatballs	4.50
served with garlic bread	

DESSERTS

Apple Pie	1.25
Lemon Tart	1.00
Cheese Cake	1.50
Ice Cream	1.00

BEVERAGES

Coca-Cola, Ginger Ale, Seven-Up	.60
Milk	.50
Coffee or Tea	.40

8. CONVERSATION

> **A:**   You're a waiter/waitress. Take B and C's order.

> **B and C:**   You're customers in a restaurant. Order what you want from the menu.

You can take orders like this:
- Are you ready to order?
- What would you like?
- ...., ... or ....?
- How would you like your ....?
- Will there be anything else?
- I'm sorry. We don't have ....

You can make suggestions like this:
- Would you care to order a drink before *lunch/dinner?*
- Would you like .... to start with?
- Something to drink?

Order what you want like this:
- Do you have ....?
- What kind of .... do you have?
- *I'll have/I'd like* .... *(with ..../but no ...., please.)*
- *Rare/Medium-rare/Medium/Well done.*
- Would you bring us *some/some more* ...., please?
- Could I have *a/an/another* ....?

Respond to a suggestion like this:
- Yes, please.
- No, thanks.
- Not right now, thank you.

9. GRAMMAR FOCUS. Fill in the blanks with the appropriate word or expression from the list. Use each one only once.

- a
- another
- no
- some
- some more

one more / several (handwritten)

WAITRESS: Are you ready to order?

WOMAN: Yes, I'll have fried chicken with peas and carrots—and I'd like ...... *some* ...... french fries.
1

WAITRESS: Would you like something to drink?

WOMAN: Not right now, thanks, but could you bring us ...... *some more* ...... bread? It's delicious.
2

WAITRESS: Certainly. And you, sir?

MAN: I'd like ...... *a* ...... hamburger with lettuce and tomato, but ...... *no* ...... onion.
3   4

WAITRESS: Anything else?

MAN: Yes. Could you bring me ...... *another* ...... napkin? This one's dirty.
5

10. FORMAL AND INFORMAL LANGUAGE.
Match each item on the left with the one on the right that means about the same. An example is given.

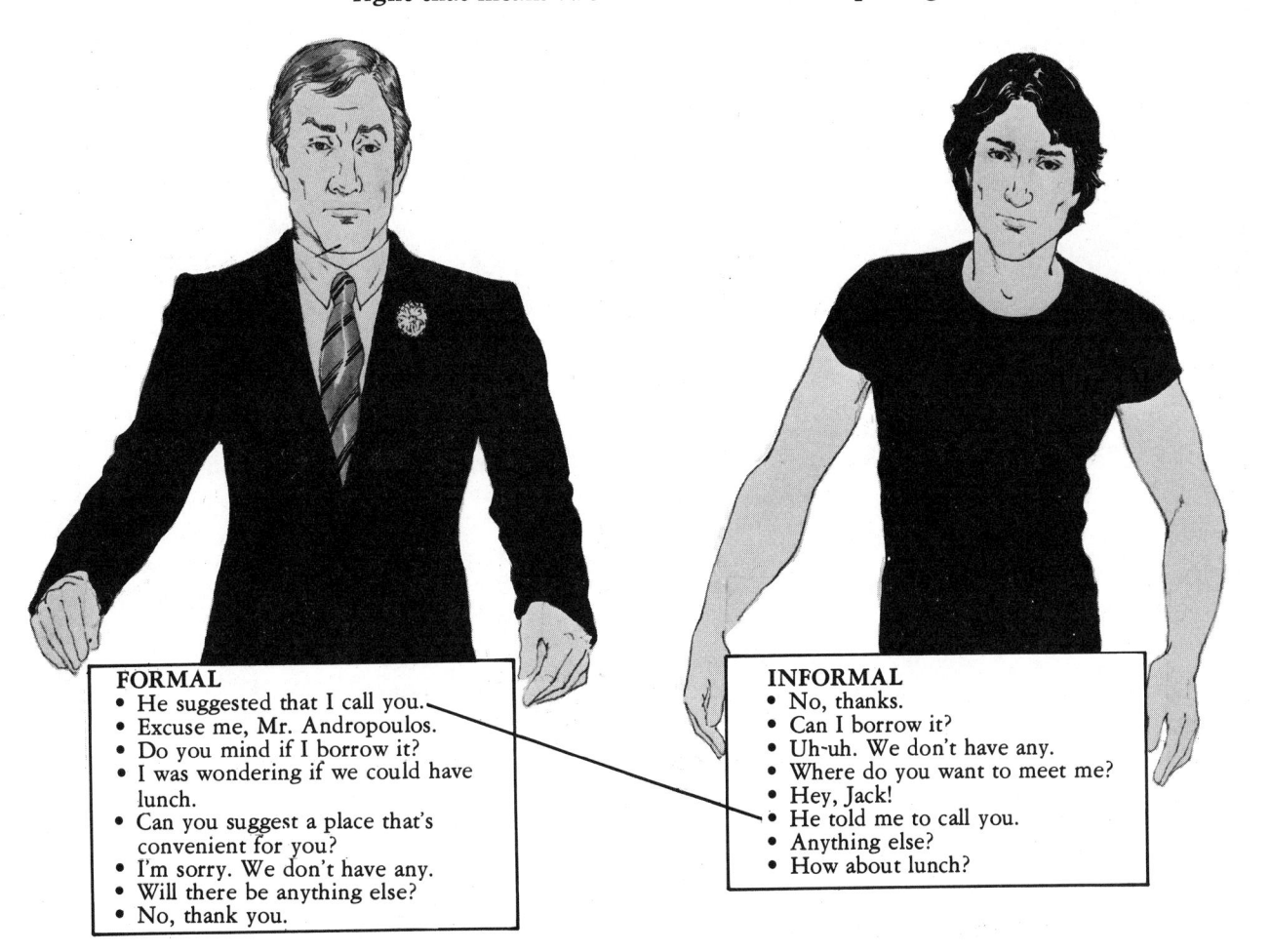

FORMAL
- He suggested that I call you.
- Excuse me, Mr. Andropoulos.
- Do you mind if I borrow it?
- I was wondering if we could have lunch.
- Can you suggest a place that's convenient for you?
- I'm sorry. We don't have any.
- Will there be anything else?
- No, thank you.

INFORMAL
- No, thanks.
- Can I borrow it?
- Uh-uh. We don't have any.
- Where do you want to meet me?
- Hey, Jack!
- He told me to call you.
- Anything else?
- How about lunch?

WOMEN IN JOURNALISM

Until very recently, women reporters wrote the women's section of the newspaper; men wrote the rest of it. Important assignments—politics, crime, foreign news—
5 are the key to money and prestige in journalism. For this reason, when women reporters are limited to "women's topics" like fashion and social events, they have no chance to advance in their profession.

10 Today, except for a few stars like Barbara Walters on TV or Oriana Fallaci in magazines and newspapers, women are still rare in the top levels of journalism. But things are beginning to change. More and
15 more women are reporting on wars, bombings and politics, and doing it as well as men. Norman Fine, the news director at WNBC-TV in New York, says "Different people have different abilities, but that
20 has nothing to do with their sex."

Sportswriting especially is opening up to women reporters. One of them is Lawrie Mifflin. In 1974, when she started to work for the New York *Daily News*, she wanted
25 to cover sports. At that time she was told that the sports department wasn't "ready for a woman reporter," but two years later Mifflin got her wish. Her editor told her "I'm not going to have you cover just women's
30 sports. If you're going to work in the sports department, you're going to do the same work as everybody else." On her third day in the department, she covered a professional basketball game.

35 Outside of sports reporting, the picture is not so good. Women are regularly refused assignments they are qualified to cover. Reporters who want to report crime or war stories are often told the assignments are
40 too dangerous for a woman. This sounds as though their editors are worried about them, but the women believe it is often just an excuse. In their fight for equal work opportunities, some women have changed
45 jobs to get better assignments; others have hired lawyers and taken legal action to get the assignments they want. B.J. Phillips, an associate editor at *Time* magazine, says the way to get results is to "Never stop pushing,
50 never stop trying, and don't be afraid to work hard. When they tell you you can't do something, ask why not. When the only answer you get is a long, embarrassed silence, you're halfway there."

**11.   READING STRATEGY: Getting the meaning from context.
Circle the answers.**

1.   *Outside of sports reporting, the picture is not so good*
     (lines 35–36) means
     a.   women only like to report sports.
     b.   women get better assignments in sports
          reporting than in other kinds of reporting.
     c.   women are not good sports photographers.

2.   *Women are regularly refused assignments they are qualified to cover*
     (lines 36–37) means
     a.   women can do the assignments well, but they
          don't get them.
     b.   women can do the assignments well, but
          they don't want them.
     c.   women can't do the assignments well.

3.   *This sounds as though their editors are worried about them,
     but the women believe it is often just an excuse*
     (lines 40–43) means
     a.   the women are worried.
     b.   the women think their editors are worried.
     c.   the women think their editors are not really
          worried.

4.   *Some women have changed jobs to get better assignments*
     (lines 44–45) means
     a.   women have gotten jobs as reporters with
          other magazines and newspapers.
     b.   women have stopped being reporters.
     c.   women have become editors.

12.   READING STRATEGY: Understanding reference words.

1.   In the article, underline what *this* (line 40) refers to.   *reporters*
2.   Underline what *this reason* (line 6) refers to.
3.   Underline what *that* (line 19) refers to.   *difference*
4.   Underline what *them* (line 22) refers to.   *women reporters*
5.   Underline what *her wish* (line 28) refers to.   *she wanted to cover sport*

13.   READING STRATEGY: Finding the main idea. Circle one.

The main idea of the article is:
a.   Women reporters now get as many important assignments as men
     reporters.
b.   More women reporters are getting important news assignments,
     but they still do not get as many as men.
c.   Women reporters don't want to do the same work as men.

REVIEW

YOU'VE LEARNED TO

identify something:	Which one? The one with the article about women journalists.
make, agree to and refuse requests:	Do you mind if I borrow it? Of course not. I'll bring it tomorrow./Sorry, I'm using it right now. Would you bring us some more butter, please?/Could I have another fork? Sure.
start a business telephone conversation:	Paula Duran. Ms. Duran, my name's Marilyn Dixon. Jack Andropoulos suggested that I call you.
offer to help:	How can I help you?
extend and accept an invitation:	I was wondering if we could have lunch sometime this week. OK.
ask for suggestions:	Where would you like to meet?/Can you suggest a place?
make, accept and reject suggestions:	How about the Red Onion on West 39th Street? Fine. Would you care to order a drink before lunch?/Something to drink? Yes, please./Not right now, thank you.
take an order and order in a restaurant:	Are you ready to order? I'd like roast beef, but no potato, please. How would you like your roast beef? Medium. Will there be anything else? Not right now, thanks.
confirm an appointment:	I'll see you there on Thursday at one o'clock.
identify someone:	Are you Paula Duran? You must be Marilyn Dixon.

GRAMMAR

That/Those

> Have you got { **that** magazine? / **those** magazines? }

Adjective Phrases and Clauses

> The one(s) { in the folder. / with the red cover(s). / (that) we were working on yesterday. }

A/An and Another

> Could I have **a** napkin?
Could I have **an** ashtray?
Could I have **another** fork?

One/Ones

> Which **one**?   The **one** in the folder.
Which **ones**?   The **ones** with the red cover(s).

Suggest + Clause

> Jack **suggested** (that) **I call you.**

Must

> You **must** be Paula Duran.

Present Perfect Progressive

> **Have** you **been waiting** long? No. I just got here.

USEFUL WORDS AND EXPRESSIONS

bring	energy	nuclear	•
mind	folder	rare	Excuse me.
order	information	well-done	How would you like
suggest	journalism	•	your _____?
wait	lunch	sometime	Not right now, thank you.
wonder	report	•	Of course not.
•	•	which	what kind of
cover	medium	•	Would you care to order a
dinner	medium-rare	before	drink?

1.   ROLE PLAY

A: You are at work. Answer the phone by saying your company's name or your name. Try to help **B**.

B: You need some information and you think **A** might be able to help you. You call **A** at work.
• When **A** answers the phone, identify yourself.
• Explain why you're calling and what you need to know.
• If necessary, make an appointment to talk after work.
  If you make an appointment, confirm the time and location.
• Say thank you and goodbye.

2.   Fill in the blanks with *a* or *an*. Put an X in the blank if there's no article.

WAITER: Good evening. ......*a*...... table for two?
1

WOMAN: Yes.

WAITER: Would you like ......*a*...... drink before
2

dinner?

WOMAN: Are you going to have ......X...... one?
3

MAN: No, I don't think so. Let's order. Do you
know what you want?

WOMAN: I think so. . . . I'll have ......X...... roast
4

beef, rare, and could I have ......X......
5

french fries instead of ......*a*...... baked
6

potato?

WAITER: Certainly. ......X...... spinach, ...X......
7   8

string beans or ......X...... carrots?
9

WOMAN: ......X...... string beans, please. And I'd
10

like ......*a*...... glass of red wine.
11

WAITER: Thank you.

MAN: I'll just have ......X...... spaghetti.
12

WOMAN: Don't you want ......*an*...... appetizer or
13

......X...... something?
14

MAN: No, I ate lunch late today.

WAITER: Will there be ......X...... anything else?
15

MAN: No, thanks. . . . Oh, yes. Would you
bring me ......*a*...... beer, please?
16

Budweiser, if you have it.

WAITER: Yes, sir.

3.   B is calling A at the office. Complete the call and say it with a partner.

A: Good morning. *(A's full name)* .

B: *(A's name)* , this is ....
I was wondering if you could lend me *that/those*
....
....

A: Which ....?

B: ....

A: Oh, yes—I know ....you mean.

B: Do you mind if ....?

A: I'm sorry. ....
right now, but ....
next ....

B: Oh, OK. That's fine. Thank you.

A: ....

B: Goodbye.

CONSOLIDATION UNIT 5 I can hardly believe it.

Why does Maria think her classmate might consider working at the Regency?
Was Maria expecting Mr. Pushkin's offer?
Does she accept it?

One afternoon Mac had arranged to meet Maria at the hotel after work. They were going to meet some friends of theirs in Greenwich Village and go to a movie. As Maria was leaving she passed Martin Pushkin, the general manager of the Regency, who was just going into his office.

"Good night, Mr. Pushkin," she said.

"Good night, Maria. . . . Oh, Maria? We're looking for a part-time bookkeeper. Do you know anyone who might be available?"

Maria thought for a minute. "As a matter of fact, I do. One of the women in my accounting class is looking for a job. I think she'd be good."

Mr. Pushkin looked interested. "Is she working now?"

"No, she's just going to school right now, but I think she'd like to work someplace where she could get experience with a computerized accounting system. If you'd like, I'll talk to her tomorrow and have her call you."

"Thanks, I'd appreciate it. By the way," he continued, "have you got a minute? I'd like to talk to you."

Maria wondered what it could be about. She knew Mac was waiting for her, but this wasn't the moment to mention it. "Yes, of course," she said.

"Good. Come in and sit down. Maria, have you decided what you're going to do when you finish your program at NYU?"

"Well, no, not yet. I'll probably go back to Mexico to work, but I don't know exactly where."

"Have you ever considered staying in New York?"

"No, I've never really thought about it. My family's in Mexico and I've always assumed I'd go back."

"Well, the reason I ask is that I'd like you to think about staying at the Regency. We've been very pleased with your work here and I think we could offer you a better position than you'd be able to find anywhere else."

This was a complete surprise to Maria and she was delighted. "Thank you very much. I'm glad you're happy with my work. . . . Could you tell me what kind of position you're thinking of?"

"Yes. We'll be needing a new assistant manager when Mr. Jenkins retires next fall and I think you'd be good at the job."

Maria tried to control her excitement. She could hardly believe it. It would be a very big promotion with a lot of responsibility. "Oh, . . . I don't know what to say—except thank you very much. Of course, I'll have to think about it."

"Of course. There's no hurry."

Mr. Pushkin stood up and reached across the desk to shake hands. Maria stood too.

"Well, feel free to come and see me if you have any questions," he said.

"Thank you, I will. Well, good night."

"Good night. See you tomorrow."

1. CONVERSATION. Talk about someone who might want a job.

A: *I'm/We're* looking for a ..... (job title) ..... Do you know anyone who ....?

B: As a matter of fact, I <u>do</u>. *My* .... /One *of my* ..../One of the .... is looking for ....

A: Is *he/she* working now?

B: Yes, *at/for* ...., but I think *he'd/she'd* rather work someplace where .... OR No, *he's/she's* ...., but I think *he'd/she'd* like to work someplace where ....

You can say:	
She's {	just studying right now.
	a housewife.
	still in school.
	between jobs.

2. CONVERSATION. Try to interest someone in a job you know about—maybe a job in your company.

A: Have you decided *what/where* you .... *when/after* ....?

B: No, not yet. I'll probably ....

A: Have you ever considered ....?

B: No, I've never really thought about it.   OR Well, yes, but ....

A: Well, the reason I ask is that ....

B: Could you tell me ....?

A: ....

You can ask for more information like this:	
Could you tell me {	what kind of position you're thinking of?
	who to talk to?
	how much they pay?
	if they have a position open now?

3. GRAMMAR REVIEW. Fill in the blanks with the superlative form of the words. The first one is done as an example.

HOW ABOUT THE REGENCY FOR YOUR ORGANIZATION'S NEXT CONVENTION?

Now, the REGENCY, ... *the largest* ..... convention hotel in New York, can offer you forty years of experience and all these benefits too:

* ..... *The best* ..... discount plans and ..... *The lowest* ..... rates available.
    1. good   2. low

* ..... *the easiest* ..... registration and ..... *the fastest* ..... check-out in town—our
    3. easy   4. fast

newly streamlined system cuts waiting time in half.

* ..... *The biggest* ..... hotel ballroom in New York for general meetings and social
    5. big

events.

* One of ..... *most flexible* ..... display areas in the city. All your exhibitors will have
    6. flexible

prime locations.

* Thirty of ..... *most* ..... conference rooms in the city.
    7. comfortable

* ..... *the most* ..... audio-visual equipment, including simultaneous transla-
    8. modern   *the most efficient*
                                                                                                      9. efficient

tion facilities in all meeting rooms.

* Four hotel restaurants to provide fast meal service, permitting .....

scheduling of convention events.

* One of ..... *the finest* ..... hotel banquet services in New York.
    10. fine

* Superlative assistance from our experienced convention staff.

Call Miss Davis at (212) 841-4000

REGENCY HOTEL
1295 Sixth Ave., New York, New York 10036

How does Mac feel about Maria's news?
Why does Maria think she might not accept the job?
What does Mac think she should do?

Mac was waiting for Maria outside the hotel. She went over and kissed him hello and they walked to the subway. "Well, what do you think?" said Mac.

"What do you mean?" she asked.

"You mean you didn't even notice? I got contacts."

"I was wondering why you weren't wearing your glasses. I knew there was something different. Hey, that's great. How do they feel?"

"OK so far. I only picked them up an hour ago."

"You look so different. Can you see OK?"

"Yeah, fine."

"Well, you look great. I'm glad you finally did it."

"Me too."

When they got to the subway station, they walked downstairs to the platform to wait for the train.

"Guess what," said Maria. "I was just talking to Mr. Pushkin—"

"Who's that?" interrupted Mac.

"The general manager at the hotel. He suggested that I stay at the Regency after I finish at NYU."

"Really? That's great. Did you ask him what your position would be?"

"Yeah, I did." She paused dramatically. "He said assistant manager."

"Are you kidding? Congratulations! Gee, that's fabulous."

Maria smiled. "Thanks. I can hardly believe it."

"So what did you tell him?"

"Well, I told him I'd have to think about it. . . . I don't know if I really want it, though."

"Why not?"

"Well, basically, because I'd rather go back to Mexico. I don't want to stay here forever. And also because at the Regency I think I'd always just be that college kid, Maria Sanchez, so I might have trouble with the staff."

"Do you really think so? 'Assistant manager' would look great on your resume, though."

"That's for sure. . . . Say, how long have we been here anyway?"

"I don't know. About ten minutes. Why?"

"It's getting late. Maybe we should've taken the bus."

"At this time of day? There's too much traffic. Anyway, the train's coming now. I can hear it."

---

4. **CONVERSATION.** Talk about what someone else suggested about your future.

A: Guess what. I was just talking to .... and *he/she* suggested that I ....
B: Really? ....?
A: Yeah. I told *him/her* ....
    I don't know if ...., though.
B: Why not?
A: Well, basically, because (*of*) ....

> *You can say:*
> Did you ask him/her .... ?

> *You can say:*
> Because { I'd rather go back to Mexico.
>   I might have trouble with the staff.
>   *of* my parents.

5. [cassette] **LISTENING. Mac and Maria are on the subway. Listen to their conversation and answer the questions.**

1. Mac is trying to persuade Maria to take the job.
   True or false?
2. Maria has decided not to take the job.
   True or false?

6. GRAMMAR REVIEW. Mac and Maria are coming out of a subway station in Greenwich Village. Fill in the blanks in their conversation. Use each item only once.

might	can't	'd better (had better)
must	could	'd rather (would rather)

MARIA: If it's a nice day tomorrow, Tomiko and I

.... ride our bikes to the Bronx
1

Zoo. Do you want to come with us? Maybe Bob or Tom would like to come too.

MAC: Thanks, but Paula asked me if I'd help her and Ray paint her living room tomorrow.

I .... go for a bike ride, though,
2

that's for sure.

MARIA: Well? .... you paint some other
3

time?

MAC: Well, . . . I'll ask her how long she thinks it'll take and call you in the morning.

MARIA: OK, but .... you call me before
4

ten? We want to leave by ten thirty or eleven.

MAC: Sure.

MARIA: Say, what time is it? It .... be
5

getting late.

MAC: Yeah. It's ten to seven.

MARIA: Already? We .... hurry. We're
6

going to be late for the movie.

7. LANGUAGE REVIEW. You're meeting a friend for lunch and you're late. Complete the conversation and say it with a partner.

YOU: Hi. Have you been waiting long?

FRIEND: As a matter of fact, ...

....

YOU: Oh, no! I'm sorry I took so long. You

must be ....

FRIEND: No, not very. I had a big breakfast. . . .

Hey, ...

today's *News*?

YOU: Sure. . . . It's here in my bag somewhere.

FRIEND: ....the want ads.

I just ....

YOU: Fired! How come?

FRIEND: .... said it was because

....

I really feel terrible.

YOU: Well, don't let..

You'll..

FRIEND: I sure hope so.

8.   READING STRATEGY: Predicting. Circle the answer.

This article is from a magazine called *New York*. Before you read the article, look at the titles and the opening quotation. You should probably read the article:
   a.   if you're curious about Eddie.
   b.   if you want information about the New York City subway system.

Brief Lives

THE MAN WHO LOVES SUBWAYS

"... on St. Patrick's Day 1977, Eddie and two friends rode the entire subway system on one fare, aiming to break the record ..."

"When I was a kid," says Edwin Rodriguez, "I used to just get on the subway and deliberately get lost and then find my way home. By the time I was five or six, I realized I could never drive a subway train; but I've always wanted nothing else, just to work for the Transit Authority." Eddie, pudgy and mustachioed, has been legally blind for almost all of his 26 years. He sees just well enough to get around unaided and with one working eye can read at very close range with a magnifying glass. And he does now work for the T.A. in its Travel Information Bureau.

Eddie speaks quietly—he is quite modest and a bit shy—but he displays an almost obsessive passion for the subway system. "I can't remember ever not being interested in it," he admits.

At 6:18 A.M. on St. Patrick's Day 1977, he and two friends embarked on a ride he had been planning since he was in high school. They rode the entire subway system on one fare, aiming to break the record of about 21 hours for this feat. For several months Eddie had been paying frequent visits to the T.A.'s headquarters—where he now works—poring over the system's schedules to devise a precisely timed itinerary. They rode on 60 trains, stopping only to rush out to a Nedick's in Queens and the men's room at Chambers Street, but the exhausting trip ended up taking 27 hours. "We were going to catch the last train out of Metropolitan Avenue to Coney Island," Eddie explains, "but we missed it because we waited at Grand Central for an *Eyewitness News* crew—they were going to meet us there at mid-

night and were late. I was very upset when I realized we wouldn't make it, but now I'm thinking of trying it again sometime."

Eddie Rodriguez grew up in Queens and has spent most of his life so far as a student at various schools for the blind. Last September his adviser at the Jewish Guild for the Blind, for which he was then working, found him his job at the T.A. Travel Information Bureau, and since then he has been answering upwards of 200 calls a day, at 330-1234.

A typical call: A traveler asks how to get from 105th Street in Canarsie to a point in Bay Ridge. Eddie's immediate response off the top of his head—he has known the entire subway map by heart since he was a boy and also knows the whole bus system of Brooklyn—impressively details not only which trains to take but how to get from one platform to the next: "Take the LL westbound from 105th Street eight stops to Myrtle Avenue. Then go upstairs and get on the M and take that all the way to Court Street. At Court Street change for the RR on the same platform, take that to Bay Ridge and walk two blocks."

Eddie seems supremely at home at this job; and in fact he is—perhaps alone among New Yorkers—loath to say a single bad word about the subway. His ambition is to work in the very complicated area of scheduling, but he is more than happy for now to be employed at the Travel Information Bureau.

Frederick Allen

9.   APPLYING READING STRATEGIES: Answer *true* or *false.*
Explain your answer.

		T	F
1.	In the future, Eddie Rodriguez hopes to drive subway trains.	T	F
2.	Eddie and his friends broke the record.	T	F
3.	Eddie can't see.	T	F
4.	Eddie has made maps for the Transit Authority.	T	F
5.	Eddie says the subway has a lot of problems.	T	F
6.	Eddie is now scheduling trains for the Transit Authority.	T	F

10. CONVERSATION. You're looking for a place in another part of town. Find out how to get there.

A:

> Ask where a place is:
>   *Do you know where* .... *is?*

B:

> Say where it is, if you know.

> If **B** knows where the place is, ask for the best way to get there.

> Give directions:
>   *Take* .... *Get off at* ....
>   *Walk* .... *blocks to* ....

> Make sure you've got the directions right. Ask **B** to repeat anything you didn't understand:
>   *Where is it again? I'd better write it down.*

> Respond:

11. WRITING SKILLS. About a year ago, when Maria filled out her application for NYU's Hotel Management Program, this was one of the questions she had to answer.

> Why do you want to go into hotel management?

These are the notes that Maria made before she started writing.

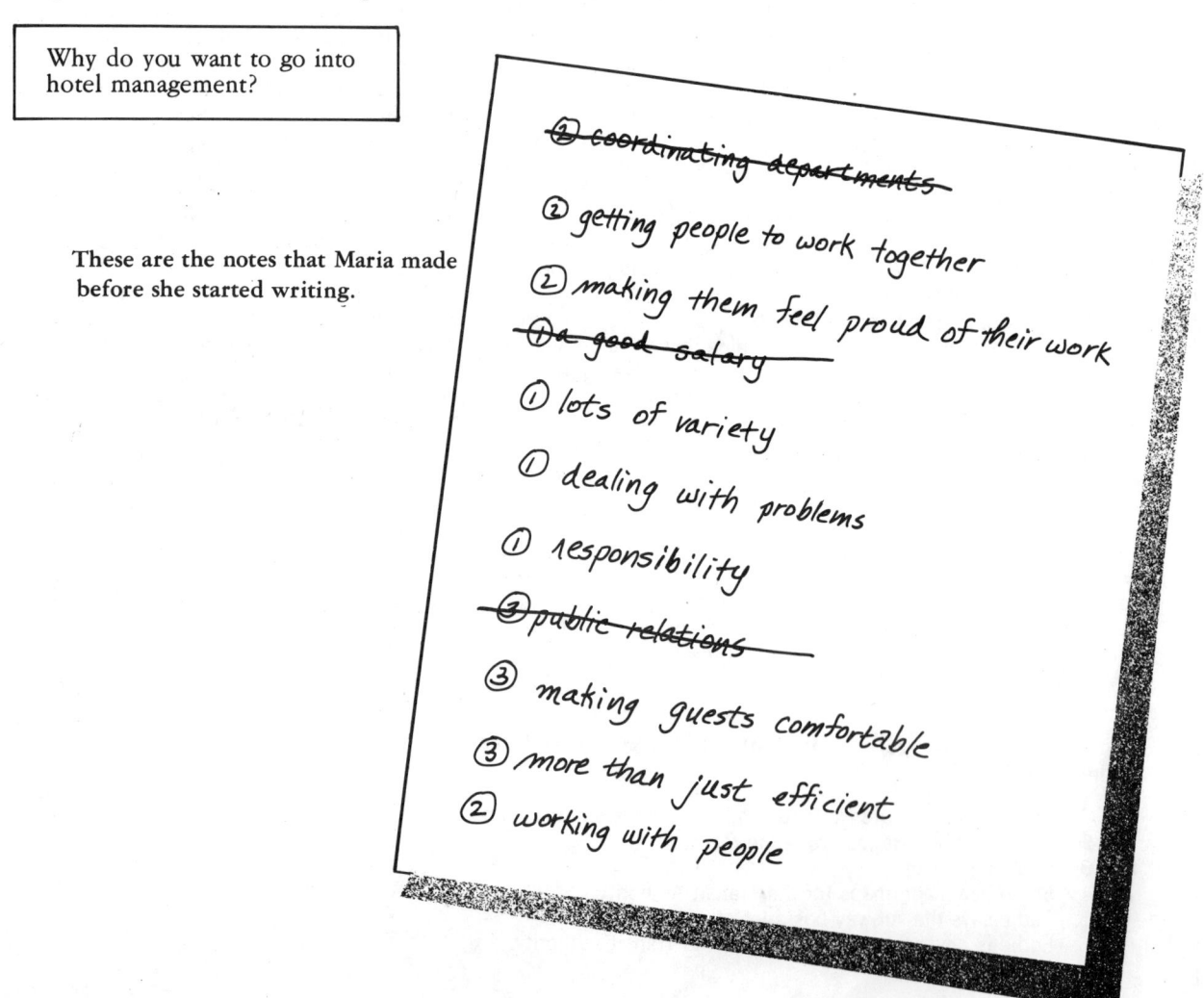

> ① ~~coordinating departments~~
> ② getting people to work together
> ② making them feel proud of their work
> ① ~~a good salary~~
> ① lots of variety
> ① dealing with problems
> ① responsibility
> ③ ~~public relations~~
> ③ making guests comfortable
> ③ more than just efficient
> ② working with people

This is how she answered the question.

> I enjoy responsibility and doing work that presents new challenges every day. I am able to deal with problems and can improvise when necessary.
>
> I also like working with people. I'm looking forward to directing a hotel staff. I think I will be able to help them work smoothly together and be proud of their work.
>
> In addition, I know that I will enjoy making my guests feel at home. I believe that in a very real sense a hotel is a home away from home. I look forward to making my hotel warm and welcoming, as well as efficient.

Answer the question below in two or three short paragraphs. First, fill in the blank in the question with the name of the career or job that interests you. Then plan, as Maria did, before you start writing:

Why do you want to go into ....?

- First, write down all your ideas. You don't need to write complete sentences at this point. Just make notes.
- Next, divide your ideas into groups of related ideas (paragraphs) by numbering them 1, 2, 3 (in other words, paragraph 1, paragraph 2, etc.).
- Then, cross out any ideas you decide not to use or add ideas to make your paragraphs more complete.
- Finally, decide on the best order for your paragraphs.
- Now write your answer to the question. While you write, you should think about the best way to express your ideas. You can add or take out ideas.

Why does Maggie mention Janet Peterson?
What day, time and place does Virginia suggest first?
What day, time and place do they finally agree on?

Maggie MacDonald was thinking of enrolling in EXCEL, a special program for returning students at Fordham University. She called the EXCEL office for information. Later, her neighbor suggested that she also talk to Virginia Kroll, a student in the program. Maggie called Mrs. Kroll at work.

VIRGINIA: Virginia Kroll.
MAGGIE: Hello. My name is Margaret MacDonald. I'm a neighbor of Janet Peterson's. She suggested that I call you.
VIRGINIA: Oh, yes. How *is* Janet? I haven't seen her for ages.
MAGGIE: She's fine. She said to tell you hello.
VIRGINIA: Good. Well, how can I help you?
MAGGIE: Well, I've decided to go back to school and I'm interested in EXCEL. I was wondering if I could come and talk to you about it sometime.

VIRGINIA: Oh, sure. That'd be fine. How about tomorrow at five? Could you come to my office?
MAGGIE: Tomorrow's fine, but I don't think I'll be able to make it at five. Do you think I could come earlier?
VIRGINIA: Let me see. . . . Would four be all right?
MAGGIE: Yes, that'd be fine.
VIRGINIA: All right. Then I'll see you here at four.
MAGGIE: Thank you very much.
VIRGINIA: Don't mention it. Goodbye.
MAGGIE: Goodbye.

12. CONVERSATION. Call someone and make an appointment.

A:

Answer the phone.

Ask how the friend is.

Comment. Then offer to help: .... *How can I help you?*

Respond and suggest a day, time and place to meet.

B:

You don't know **A**, but you want to apply for a job where **A** works. Identify yourself. Mention the friend who suggested that you call: .... *suggested that I call you.*

Answer.

Tell **A** what you need and request an appointment: *I've been thinking about .... and I was wondering if ....*

Agree on the time or suggest another time: *Yes, that'd be fine.* OR *Well, I don't think I'll be able to .... Do you think ....?*

When you have both agreed on when to meet, end the conversation.

13. GRAMMAR REVIEW. Maggie went to see Virginia Kroll the next day. They had a long talk about EXCEL. Fill in the blanks with the appropriate words from the list.

can I	do you know	do you think	why don't you	I'd like to
so I can	you might not be able to	would you like to	I wish I'd	if you can

MAGGIE: Oh, I knew there was something I forgot to ask. ....1........................... if I can just take a couple of courses first, or do I have to start studying for a degree right away?

VIRGINIA: Well, I really don't know. ....2...................... ask them ....3................... do that when you go to register?

MAGGIE: That's a good idea. ....4..................... start out with two or three background courses, like math or business English and then begin the degree program next semester. By the way, ...5................... there's still room? I mean, I won't have any trouble getting in, will I?

VIRGINIA: No, I don't think so. It *is* kind of late to register for this semester, so ....6................... get into all the courses you want.

MAGGIE: Yeah, well, I just want to take a few courses now ....7................... see how I like going to school again. . . . Well, I really have to go. It was very nice meeting you. ....8................... talked to you sooner. You've been a great help.

VIRGINIA: Oh, it was a pleasure and it was really nice meeting *you*. When are you going to register?

MAGGIE: Tomorrow.

VIRGINIA: Well, ...9................... get together for coffee after my last class, say at three?

MAGGIE: OK. That would be nice. ....10................... meet you at the EXCEL office?

VIRGINIA: Sure. I'll see you tomorrow, then.

MAGGIE: OK. Bye.

UNIT 6 George had an accident, but he's going to be all right.

People alive today

The American Red Cross awards Certificates of Merit to people who use its emergency procedures to save a life. Several thousand people who might have died are alive today. Meet some of them.

1. READING STRATEGY:
Recognizing the author's purpose.

This article was probably written:
a. because the Red Cross wanted to do something nice for Susan Morris, Paul Peloquin and Peter Gerow.
b. to teach readers how to save lives during emergencies.
c. to make readers aware that Red Cross emergency procedures have saved many lives.

Explain why you answered as you did.

From *National Geographic Magazine*, June 1981.

NEXT-DOOR neighbors (*left*) Peter Palermo, 50 (*center*), and Frank Gerow, 48 (*right*), live in Alexandria, Virginia, and often help each other with projects like building the Gerows' patio roof. Now there is a new bond between them. They have both had heart attacks. And they are both alive today because of Frank's 19-year-old son, Pete (*left*), who has received two Red Cross Certificates of Merit for his rescues.

Both men were stricken suddenly, just four months apart. Their hearts had stopped and they weren't breathing. Pete kept them alive with cardiopulmonary resuscitation (CPR)—a lifesaving procedure that combines mouth-to-mouth breathing with external chest compressions—until the arrival of paramedics.

"I was too busy to be scared," said Pete. "It was only afterward—I had trouble sleeping for a while."

home plate, bounced up and jabbed him in the neck. He staggered to the third baseline, then fell unconscious. Paul Peloquin (*right*), an athletic trainer, rushed over and found that McKenna had stopped breathing.

"I remembered that he had been chewing tobacco," said Paul, "and I realized that it was lodged in his throat." Working quickly, Paul cleared the obstruction, letting the umpire breathe normally again.

Susan Morris, ten (*below, right*), of Tullahoma, Tennessee, is fortunate enough to have a dad, a Red Cross first-aid instructor, who taught her about water safety. When her friend Dwyne Ellis, 12 (*left*), slipped off a docked motorboat in a lake and started to go under, Susan knew she should try to reach for her first—and not go in the water herself. She jumped to a lower boat, where she could hold on to Dwyne's arm and keep her head above water while shouting for help.

A hundred years ago American Red Cross Founder Clara Barton had a dream of people helping people in time of need. Today, in people like Susan Morris, Paul Peloquin, and Pete Gerow, that dream lives on.

"Strike two!" John McKenna (*above*, in cap) of New Bedford, Massachusetts, was umpiring a high school baseball game when a curveball hit

2. READING STRATEGIES: Skimming and predicting. You want to find out more about the life-saving procedures used by Susan Morris, Paul Peloquin and Pete Gerow. Some of these pamphlets contain the information you need. Read enough of each pamphlet to decide whether you should take it or not. Do not read more than necessary. Mark each pamphlet at the place where you stopped reading.

Play it ..
Work it .
Live it ..

SAFE!

According to the National Safety Council, there are approximately 100,000 accidental deaths in the U.S. every year. Many of these tragic deaths could be avoided if people followed simple safety rules and took basic precautions against accidents in the home, on the road, in the workplace—and even in public parks and playgrounds.

By far, the highest number of accidental deaths in the U.S. are due to traffic accidents. Nearly 150 million people drive in this country, so it is not surprising that annually there are about 50,000 fatal accidents involving motor vehicles.

WHEN SOMEONE IS BLEEDING BADLY

DON'T JUST STAND THERE

The human body can tolerate the loss of up to two quarts of blood, but severe bleeding can lead to death in a few minutes.

Here are several procedures you can follow to stop heavy bleeding:

1. DIRECT PRESSURE
Fold a cloth into a thick pad (preferably a clean cloth, although any rag, a piece of paper or even the palm of your hand will do in a pinch). Apply whatever you're using to the entire surface of the wound and press down. If the cloth becomes soaked with blood, apply another (and as many more as necessary) and press down harder on the wound.

CARDIAC ARREST

It strikes three out of every thousand people in this country annually. If it happened to someone you know—or to a stranger—would you know what to do?

Experts say about one-fifth of heart attack victims could be saved if someone would quickly apply cardio-pulmonary resuscitation (CPR).

If you find someone unconscious and you suspect that his or her heart has stopped:

1. Have someone call for medical help immediately. A few seconds can mean the difference between life and death when a heart stops beating.
2. If you are alone, you will have to administer both mouth-to-mouth artificial breathing and exterior heart massage.

REACH
THROW
ROW
GO

Every year thousands of Americans die by drowning. Some of these tragic deaths occur when someone tries to save a person who is having trouble in the water. The would-be hero swims out, only to be pulled down by the frightened victim.

The basic rule to remember when trying to save someone from drowning is never to swim out to a person until you have tried everything else.

REMEMBER THIS ORDER:

1. REACH
If the person is near the edge of a dock, river, small boat, etc., hold on to a firm object, reach out, and hold on to him or her. If the person is too far out for you to reach, use a pole, branch or other strong object. If the person is too heavy to pull out, shout for help.

Tarrytown Comm Hosp
Rm 311
leave sta. and left
right on Main
left on Broadway
right at Bank N.Y.

Where's George?
What's wrong with him?
How is Mac getting to the hospital?

MAGGIE: Mac, I just wanted to let you know that George is in the hospital. He had an accident at work—

MAC: Oh, no!

MAGGIE: —but he's OK. He's got a broken leg and a couple of broken ribs, but he's going to be all right.

MAC: What happened?

MAGGIE: He fell from the second story where they were working.

MAC: Oh, no! Where is he now?

MAGGIE: He's in Tarrytown Community Hospital.

MAC: Listen, I'll catch the next train.

MAGGIE: No, that's not necessary. You can't see him tonight anyway—he's sleeping now—and Billy and I are fine. Why don't you come tomorrow? I can meet you at the station if you tell me what time.

MAC: Well, I'm not sure what time I'll get there. I'll have to check the train schedule. Is the hospital within walking distance?

MAGGIE: Yeah. It's only eight or nine blocks from the station.

MAC: OK. Let me get a pencil. . . . What's the name of the hospital again?

MAGGIE: Tarrytown Community. He's in Room 311.

MAC: OK. How do I get there?

MAGGIE: When you leave the station, turn left. Walk to the corner and turn right on Main Street.

MAC: Uh-huh.

MAGGIE: Walk five or six blocks to Broadway and turn left again. After you walk about two blocks, turn right. I don't remember the name of the street, but there's a bank on the corner. The Bank of New York.

MAC: Wait a minute. I turn *right* at the bank?

MAGGIE: Uh-huh.

MAC: OK.

MAGGIE: The hospital's on that street, on your left. You can't miss it.

MAC: OK, let me see if I've got that right. I turn left when I leave the station and right on Main Street. Then left on Broadway and right again at the bank?

MAGGIE: That's right. OK, I guess I'll see you tomorrow.

MAC: Right. And you take it easy, OK?

MAGGIE: I will, Mac. Thanks. And I'll tell George you're coming.

3.   ROLE PLAY

A: You're in New York City. You are going to meet **B** in Tarrytown at the place where he/she works so you can go visit George together.

Find out and write down:
- where **B** works.
- how to get there from the train station.

B: You work in Tarrytown at one of the places on the map on page 61. **A** is going to meet you there so you can go visit George together. Give **A** directions from the station. Use the map.

A: Let me get a *pencil/piece of paper.* . . . OK. What's the name of the place again?

B: ....

A: OK. How do I get there?

B/A: (*Give and write down directions.*)

A: OK, let me see if I've got that right. I ....?

B: That's right.   OR   No, ...

You can give directions like this:

When you leave the station, turn **left**.
Walk **six** blocks and turn **left** on Broadway.
Walk **two** blocks and turn **right**. I don't remember the name of the street, but the library's on the corner (there's a *bank* on the corner).

You can ask for clarification like this:

What was the name of the street/store/etc. (again)?
Wait a minute. I turn **right** at the bank?

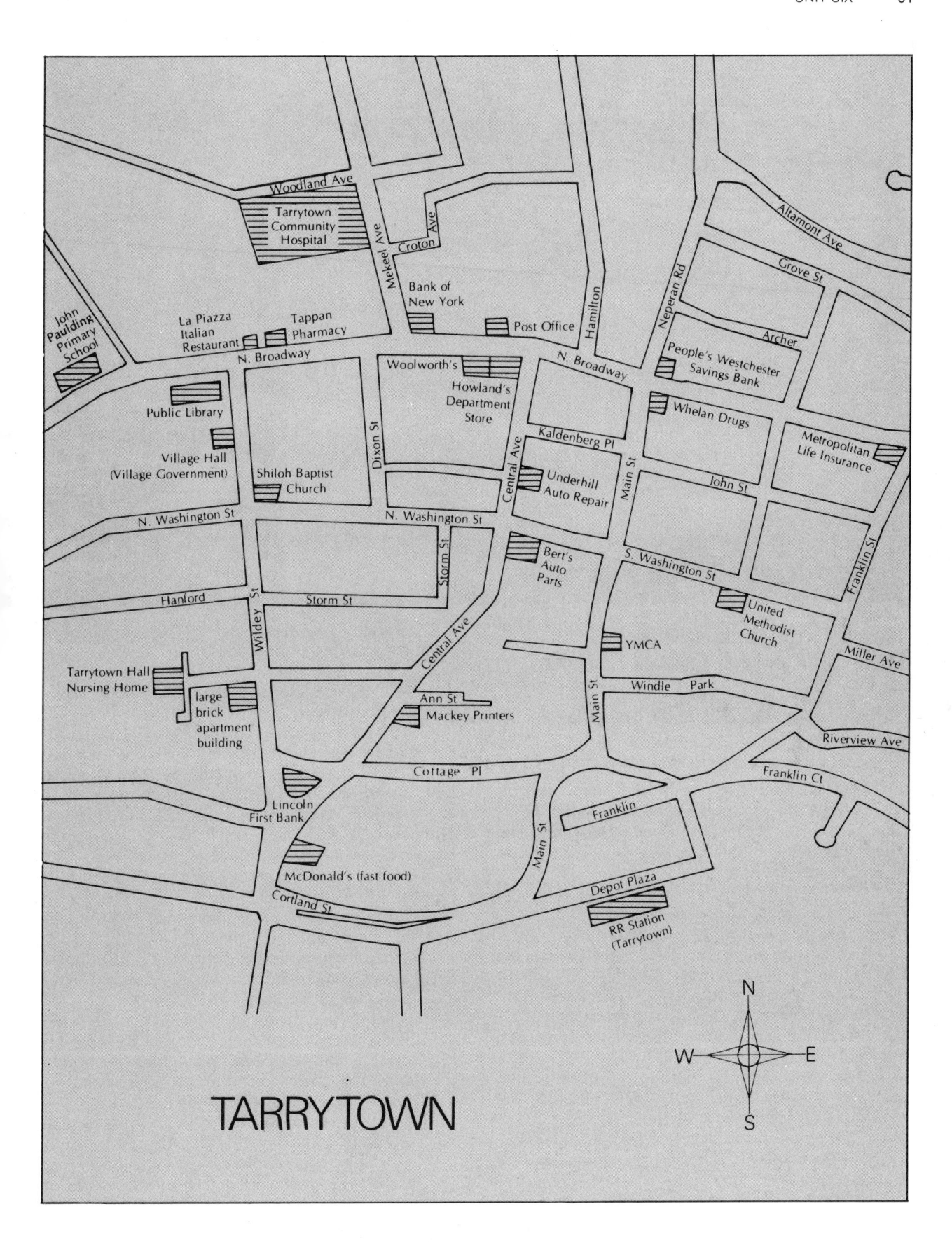

TARRYTOWN

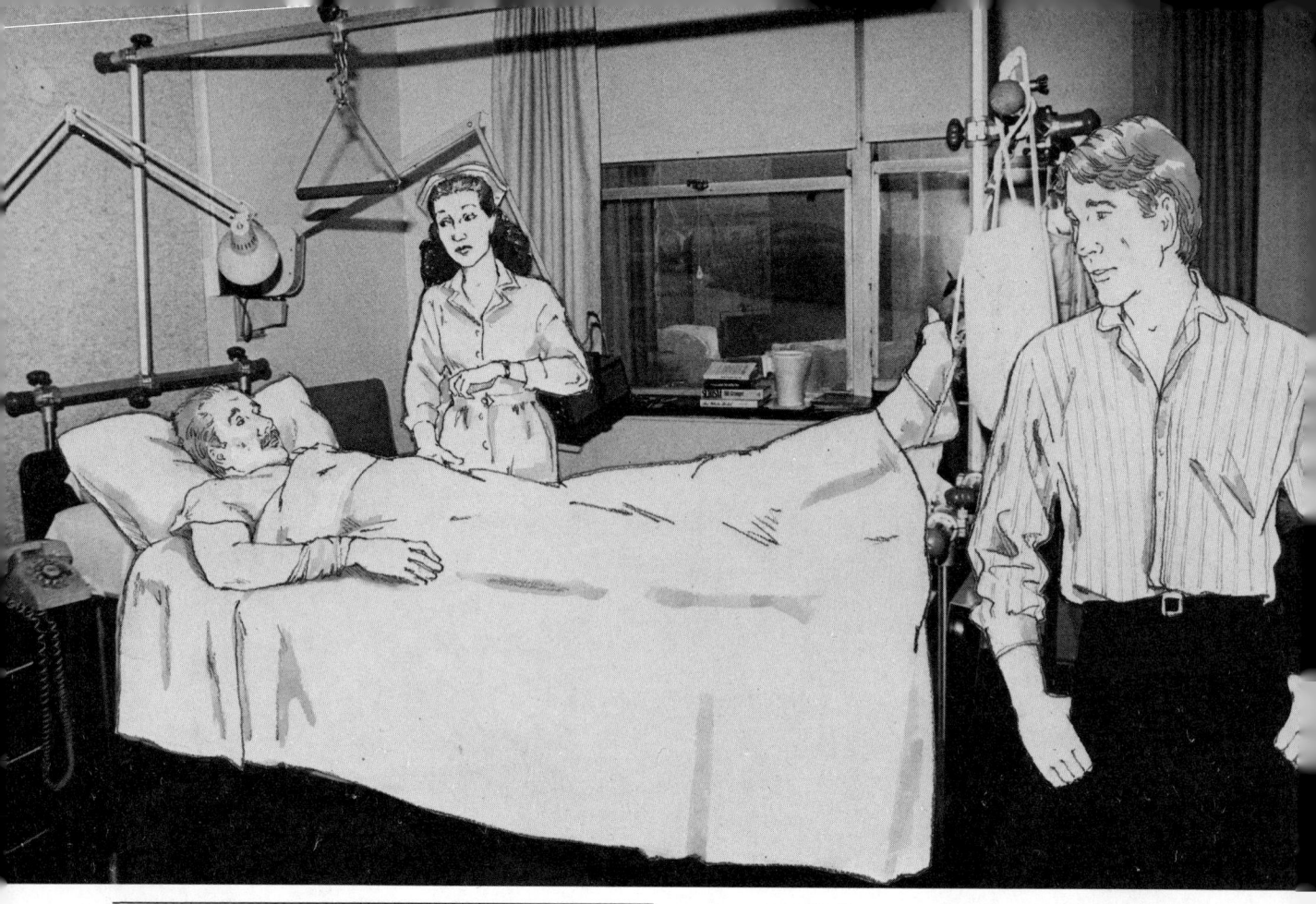

How did the accident happen?
How did George's parents take the news?
What does Mac think of his new roommate?

Mac had wanted to get to the hospital early to see George, but his new roommate, Larry Allen, called and asked if he could move in that morning. There wasn't anyone Mac could leave a key with, so he had to wait for him.

When Mac finally got to the hospital, he found George looking better than he'd expected.

"How are you feeling?" Mac asked him.

George smiled weakly. "Not too well yet. My ribs still hurt every time I breathe."

"What about your leg?"

"Actually, that doesn't hurt too much anymore."

"Well, I'm glad you're OK. How'd it happen anyway?" asked Mac.

"Oh, I was checking some work on the second story and . . . well, somehow I slipped and fell. The next thing I knew I was in the hospital."

"You're lucky you weren't killed," said Mac.

"Yeah, I know," said George, looking a little embarrassed.

"Have you talked to Mom and Dad yet?"

"Maggie called them last night. I only talked to them for a couple of minutes."

"What did they say?"

"Well, they didn't seem too upset. They said I should've been more careful—"

"That's for sure," interrupted Mac.

"—and that I shouldn't go back to work too soon. I told them they didn't need to worry about *that,* not the way *I'm* feeling."

Mac smiled sympathetically. "I can imagine. How long do you think you'll have to stay in the hospital?"

"I don't know yet. Not too long, I hope. But I suppose I'll be on crutches for a while. The doctor said I'll have to wear a cast for at least eight weeks. Anyway, what's new with you?"

"Well, my new roommate moved in this morning. I don't know, but I think we're going to have trouble getting along."

"What do you mean?"

"Well, he called to say he wanted to bring his stuff over at eight—and then he didn't get there until ten thirty! That's why I couldn't get here earlier."

"Did he know you were going out?"

"Yeah. When he called, I told him you were in the hospital."

"Maybe he couldn't help it."

"I don't know. But he didn't even apologize or anything. I got the impression he just didn't care."

4.   CONVERSATION. Tell someone how your accident happened.

A: How are you feeling?

B: Not too well.   OR   Much better.

A: *I bet./That's good.* How did it happen anyway?

B: I .... and ....

A: You're lucky ....

> **B** *can tell about the accident like this:*
>
> I slipped and fell.
> I was crossing the street and got hit by a car.
> This guy went through a red light and hit me.
> My car skidded and hit a tree.

> **A** *can comment like this:*
>
> You're lucky (that) $\begin{cases} \text{you weren't killed.} \\ \text{it wasn't any worse.} \\ \text{you didn't hurt your back.} \\ \text{somebody was there.} \end{cases}$

"My car skidded and hit a tree."

"This guy went through a red light and hit me."

"I slipped and fell."

5.   CONVERSATION. Continue talking about the accident above. Discuss what someone else (for example, B's boss, parents, husband, wife, etc.) said about it.

A: Have you talked to .... yet?

B: Yeah, I *talked to/saw* .... *last night/ yesterday/*etc.

A: What did .... say?

B: Well, *he/she/they seemed pretty/didn't seem too* .... said I *should/shouldn't/ should've/shouldn't have* ....

> *You can say:*
>
> They seemed pretty upset.
> They didn't seem too worried.
>
> They said $\begin{cases} \text{I should take better care of myself.} \\ \text{I shouldn't go back to work too soon.} \\ \text{I should've been more careful.} \\ \text{I shouldn't have been so careless.} \end{cases}$

6.   GRAMMAR FOCUS. Mac and George are continuing their conversation in the hospital. Fill in the blanks with *should, shouldn't, should've,* or *shouldn't have* and the correct form of the verb.

MAC: You know, I'm really having a hard time finding a job in engineering. I might have to start looking for something else.

GEORGE: Oh, come on. You haven't even graduated yet. I think you ___*should keep*___ looking.
1. keep

MAC: Well, maybe so, but now I wish I'd studied harder. I ___*shouldn't have gone out*___ so much last semester. With *my* grades, I don't
2. go out

know if I can get the type of job I want.

GEORGE: You think you ___*should have stayed*___ home and studied the night you met Maria?
3. stay

MAC: Come on, George. You know what I mean.

GEORGE: Well, anyway, you ___*shouldn't worry*___ about it too much. You'll get a job. You'll see.
4. worry

MAC: I hope you're right.

7. 🔲 **LISTENING. While George was in the hospital, lots of people called to ask how he was. One of them was his neighbor, Marty Peterson. Listen to their phone conversation and circle the answers.**

1. How does George feel today?
    a. Worse.   b. About the same.   c. Better.
2. How does George feel about being in the hospital?
    a. He hates it.   b. He doesn't mind it.   c. He doesn't want to go home.
3. What was the main reason for Marty Peterson's call?
    a. To be friendly.   b. To offer help.   c. To find out about the accident.

8. **CONVERSATION**

> **A:**   You just heard about **B**'s accident.

> **B:**   You recently had an accident. Tell **A** how you're feeling.

A: I just heard about your accident. How are you doing?
B: Much better, thanks. My .... *don't/doesn't* hurt too much anymore.   OR   Not too well yet. My .... still *hurt/hurts*.
A: How long *do/are* ....?
B: Probably *until/for* ....
A: Well, *I'm glad/I hope* ....
B: ....

> *You can say:*
>
> How long $\begin{cases} \text{do you have to wear that cast?} \\ \text{are you going to be in the hospital?} \end{cases}$

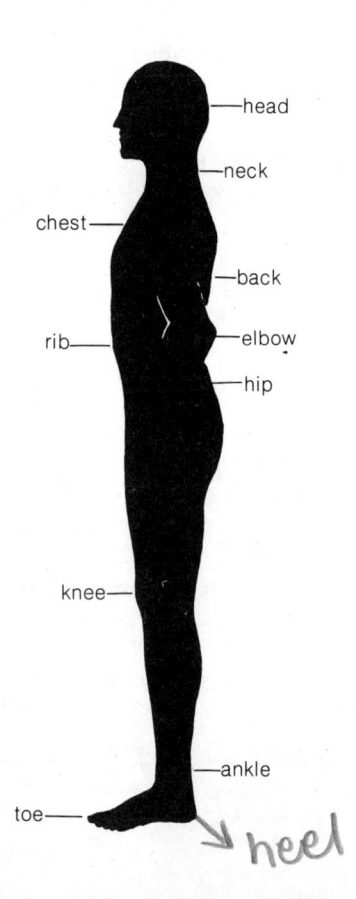

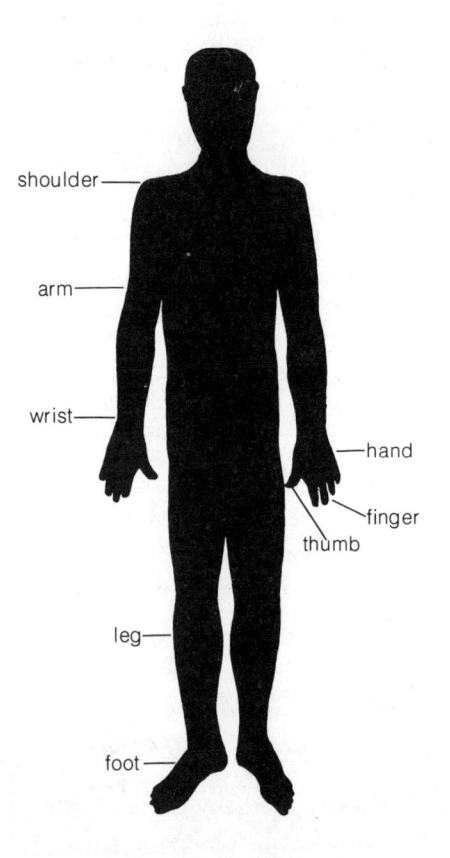

PHILADELPHIA MUTUAL ACCIDENT/ILLNESS INSURANCE CLAIM

PLEASE PRINT ALL INFORMATION

1. NAME OF INSURED PERSON
George MacDonald

2. SEX M
3. DATE OF BIRTH Sept. 22, 1948

5. ADDRESS
79 Fairview Ave., Tarrytown, NY 10591

4. IDENTIFICATION NUMBER ZA9325

7. NAME OF EMPLOYER
Perretti Construction Co.

6. TELEPHONE NO. (914) 631-0648

9. EMPLOYER'S ADDRESS
150 Main St., Tarrytown, NY 10591

8. POSITION Foreman

10. BUSINESS TELEPHONE NO. (914) 631-1539

11. IF ACCIDENT, DESCRIBE CIRCUMSTANCES (at work, at home, traveling from home to work, etc.) GIVE EXACT LOCATION, CONDITIONS AND SEQUENCE OF EVENTS. The accident occurred while I was at work at a building under construction at 450 South Broadway, Tarrytown, NY. It was raining and I slipped on a girder on the second story, lost my balance and fell to the ground.

12. NATURE OF ILLNESS OR INJURY
Broken leg and three broken ribs.

13. WHEN WAS ILLNESS FIRST NOTICED OR WHEN DID ACCIDENT HAPPEN?
about 4:00 p.m., April 29, 1980.

14. AUTHORIZATION (READ CAREFULLY BEFORE SIGNING): I hereby authorize any physician, hospital, insurance company, employer, public or private organization to release any information regarding the medical history, treatment, disability, or benefits payable for this claim to the Philadelphia Mutual Insurance Company or its representatives. A photocopy of this claim and authorization form shall be as valid as the original.

SIGNATURE OF INSURED PERSON
George MacDonald   DATE May 1, 1980

15. NAME AND ADDRESS OF DOCTOR(S) TREATING INSURED PERSON FOR ILLNESS OR INJURY
NAME
NAME
ADDRESS
ADDRESS

16. DATES OF TREATMENT

18. DATES OF HOSPITALIZATION
FROM ____ 19 ____ THROUGH ____ 19 ____

17. WAS INSURED PERSON HOSPITALIZED?
YES ____ NO ____

PHYSICIAN'S SIGNATURE

19. NAME AND ADDRESS OF HOSPITAL
DATE

MAIL THIS FORM TO: Philadelphia Mutual Insurance Company, Claims Department
3300 Walnut Street, Philadelphia, PA 19104

George had a lot of forms to fill out as a result of his accident. One of the insurance forms included this item.

11. IF ACCIDENT, DESCRIBE CIRCUMSTANCES (at work, at home, traveling from home to work, etc.) GIVE EXACT LOCATION, CONDITIONS AND SEQUENCE OF EVENTS.

George planned his answer to the item like this:

circumstances - at work

location - building under construction at 450 South Broadway, Tarrytown, N.Y.

conditions - raining

events - slipped on girder, and fell from 2nd story

This is the way George's answer looked after he wrote it.

The accident occurred while I was at work at a building under construction at 450 South Broadway, Tarrytown, NY. It was raining and I slipped on a girder on the second story, lost my balance and fell to the ground.

9. WRITING SKILLS. Describe an accident you have had. Plan and write your description the way George did.

YOU'VE LEARNED TO

ask someone to repeat something:	What's the name of the place again?
ask for and give directions:	How do I get there?
	When you leave the station, turn left. Walk two blocks and turn right.
	I don't remember the name of the street, but there's a bank on the corner.
ask for and give confirmation:	OK, let me see if I've got that right. I turn right at the bank?
	That's right.
make a request:	Let me get a pencil.
	Wait a minute.
talk about how someone's feeling:	How are you feeling?/How are you doing?
	Much better. My leg doesn't hurt too much anymore./Not too well. My ribs still hurt.
	Well, I'm glad you're OK.
talk about an accident:	How did it happen anyway?
	I was checking some work on the second story and I slipped and fell.
	You're lucky you weren't killed.
ask if someone has done something:	Have you talked to Mom and Dad yet?
ask about and report a conversation:	What did they say?
	They didn't seem too upset. They said I should've been more careful.
talk about how long something will continue:	How long are you going to be in the hospital?
	Probably until Wednesday./Not too long, I hope.

GRAMMAR

Past Tense: Relationship of Tenses

> I **was checking** some work and I **slipped** and **fell.**

Should and Should have

Present:	
They said	I **should** take better care of myself.
	I **shouldn't** go back to work too soon.

Past:	
They said	I **should've been** more careful.
	I **shouldn't have been** so careless.

Present Perfect with Yet

Have you talked to Mom and Dad **yet?**	Maggie called them last night.

Until

How long are you going to be in the hospital?	Probably **until** next week.

Still/Anymore

> My ribs **still** hurt.
> My back doesn't hurt **anymore.**

USEFUL WORDS AND EXPRESSIONS

cross	turn	station	left
fell (fall)	wear	•	•
happen	•	careful	until
hit	accident	careless	•
hurt	back	lucky	how long
kill	cast	worried	•
seem	guy	worse	I'll bet.
skid	hospital	•	take care of
slip	library	anymore	Wait a minute.
	piece	anyway	

1. **GRAMMAR REVIEW. Mac visited George again the next day. Fill in the blanks in their conversation with words from the list. Use each item once.**

anymore	pretty soon	until	yet
how long	still	when	

MAC: .... are you going to be here anyway?
                              1

GEORGE: I don't know .... I have to stay ....
                              2   3
         they can change the cast. I hope that'll be ....
                                                      4
         I feel a lot better today and I don't have a fever ....
                                                             5

MAC: Well, that's good. I talked to Maria this morning. She sends her best.

GEORGE: Thanks. Is she .... at that hotel? What is it? The Regent?
                            6

MAC: The Regency. Yeah. In fact .... she finishes her training
                                       7
         program, she might get a job there.

GEORGE: Oh, that's great. Say hello to her for me, OK?

MAC: Sure.

2. **Fill in the blanks with** *should, shouldn't, should have* **or** *shouldn't have* **and the correct form of the verb.**

Is Mary right or wrong? She's right. You

.... someone who has
         1. move

had an accident.

You .... for help
              2. call

immediately.

Did Dan do the right thing? No, he didn't! He

.... after his friend.
         1. go

Instead, he .... the life
                 2. throw

preserver or used the boat.

3.   ROLE PLAY

A: Ask **B** how to get somewhere. Write down **B**'s directions. Ask **B** to repeat anything you don't understand.	**B:** Give **A** directions to a place.

4.   Complete the conversation and say it with a partner.

A: I just heard about .... How is ....?

B: .... still ....,

but ....

A: Well, I'm glad .... How did it happen anyway?

B: ....

really should've/shouldn't have ....

A: Yeah, ...'s lucky ....

How long ....?

B: Probably until ....

UNIT 7 Could you give Mac a message for me?

Why does Maria agree to work overtime?
Why does she have to call Mac?
Why does Maria think that Larry is rude?

Late one afternoon Maria was getting ready to leave work when the assistant manager, Mr. Jenkins, came looking for her.

"Maria, could you do me a favor? Anita just called in sick. Could you stay until nine tonight?"

"Gee, I'm sorry. I can't." Maria had a date with Mac at seven, but she'd already said no two or three times that month when she'd been asked to work overtime. "But I might be able to stay until seven thirty, if that's any help."

"Yeah, that would help," he said.

"OK, I'll let you know for sure as soon as I make a phone call."

"Thanks a lot. I really appreciate it."

Maria picked up the phone and dialed Mac's number. She let the phone ring several times and was about to hang up when Mac's roommate answered.

"Hello?"

"Hi, Larry. This is Maria. Is Mac there?"

"No, he isn't."

"Do you know when he'll be back?"

"Uh-uh."

Maria thought Larry sounded annoyed. At any rate, he certainly wasn't being very friendly. "Well, could you give him a message for me?" she asked.

"I'm not going to see him. I'm going out."

"Well . . . uh . . . could you just leave him a note? I'm meeting him for dinner and I want to tell him I'm going to be late."

"Yeah. I guess so. Wait a minute. Let me get a pencil. . . . All right, what is it?"

"Just tell him I'll be half an hour late tonight. Oh—and would you ask him to bring my umbrella? I left it there the other day."

"Yeah, OK."

"And could you please leave the note on his desk so he'll be sure to see it?"

"Yeah. Anything else?"

"No. That's all. Thanks a lot," she said.

"Yeah. Bye."

"Goodb—"

Larry hung up the phone before Maria finished saying goodbye. She stood there a moment wondering why he'd been so rude. Then she shrugged and decided to forget it. She went to tell Mr. Jenkins she could stay.

1.   CONVERSATION

> **A:**   You have a problem and you need a favor. Ask **B** to do something for you.

> **B:**   You can't do what **A** wants, but you might be able to do something else to help.

A: ...., could you do me a favor?   *(Explain your problem.)*.... Could you ....?

B: Gee, I'm sorry I can't. But I might be able to ...., if that's any help.

A: Yeah, that would help.   OR   No, I'm afraid it isn't. But thanks anyway.

> *You can say:*
> I'll let you know for sure . . .
> . . . { after lunch.
>   after I talk to my mother.
>   as soon as I make a phone call.
>   as soon as I can.

*If **A** accepts your offer, continue like this:*

B: OK. I'll let you know for sure *after/ as soon as* I ....

A: Thanks a lot. I really appreciate it.

2.   GRAMMAR FOCUS. After Maria called Mac's apartment, she reported back to the assistant manager. Fill in the blanks as in the example.

MARIA: Mr. Jenkins—

MR. JENKINS: Just a second, Maria. I'll be with you as soon as ....*I write*.... this

                       write

        down. . . . OK. What's the word? Can you stay?

MARIA: Yes, I can.

MR. JENKINS: Great. Why don't you take a break now? Then after ....*you get back*....

                1. get back

I'd like you to take these bills over to the accounting office.

MARIA: OK. Do you want anything from the coffee shop?

MR. JENKINS: No, thanks. I'm leaving as soon as ....*finish*.... this report.

           2. finish

MARIA: OK. I'll be back soon.

3. CONVERSATION. Ask someone to give a message to someone else.

A: Could you give .... a message for me?
B: Sure.
A: Tell *him/her* .... OR Ask *him/her* to
....
B: Yeah, OK. Anything else?
A: No, that's all. Thanks a lot.
B: You're welcome.

<table>
<tr><td colspan="2">You can say: a moment</td></tr>
<tr><td>Tell him (that)</td><td>{ I'll be late.
Maria called.
I'm working late. }</td></tr>
<tr><td>Ask him to</td><td>{ bring my umbrella.
call me at work.
wait for me. }</td></tr>
</table>

4. LISTENING. Just before she left the hotel, Maria went into Mr. Jenkins's office to leave some papers on his desk. As she was walking out of his office the phone rang. Listen and write down the message.

#1 BEST SELLER

"A DOCUMENTARY MASTERPIECE . . .
When future historians want to know what life was
like in twentieth century America, they will have to
consult Studs Terkel's newest book. . . . An
5 extraordinary mosaic of American work and life."

SATURDAY REVIEW

For three years Studs Terkel criss-crossed
America, interviewing workers—all kinds of
workers—to find out how they feel about their jobs
10 and themselves. *Working* is the result.

"STRIKING . . . TERKEL HAS CAUGHT THE
SOUND OF THE PEOPLE . . . A record of 'real'
people and 'real' thoughts and everyday events and
moods that may someday help to create a fuller
15 picture of what our times were all about."

BALTIMORE SUN

FRANCES SWENSON

*A bungalow in a lower-middle-class neigh-
borhood in the city. A widow, she lives with her
grown son. "How would I describe myself? A
20 happy-go-lucky, middle-aged woman." (Laughs.)
She is a switchboard operator at a large motel
frequented by conventioneers. She has had this job for
three years, though she has been a telephone operator
for at least fifteen.*

25 You have to have a nice, smiling voice. You
can't be angry or come in like you've been out the
night before. (Laughs.) You always have to be
pleasant, no matter how bad you feel.

I had one gentleman the other day and he
30 wanted an outside call. I asked his name and room
number, which we have to charge to his room. And
he says "What's it to you?" I said "I'm sorry, sir,
this is our policy." And he gets a little hostile. But
you just take it with a grain of salt and you just keep
35 on working. Inside you and in your head you get
mad. But you still have to be nice when the next call
comes in. There's no way to let it out. I'm pretty
easy to get along with. I'm not the type to get angry
on the phone.

40 First thing I do is get my headset on, and I sit
down at the board to relieve the girl that's been
working all night. This is a board that's twenty-four
hours. It's the type of chair that a stenographer
would sit on. Believe me, after eight hours it's not a
45 comfortable chair. (Laughs.) We are constantly
kept busy. There isn't an idle moment. There's not
much time to converse. I have worked in different
offices and you can even take the chance to pick up
a crochet hook, to keep your fingers busy. Not
50 here.

A lot of men don't realize what a switchboard
is and how complicated they are. We had one of the
young men—an assistant manager trainee—he
worked just the lunch hour, and he had it. You got
55 to memorize all the departments. You can't keep
looking at your sheets. You gotta remember these
things.

The kids today don't work like the older
women. They take a job as it comes. If they want to
60 work, they work. If they don't, they fool around.
We have a couple that sit on the phone half of the
day, take time out. That puts the burden on the rest
of the girls. The older women are more loyal,
they're more conscientious. They don't take time
65 off.

Want to hear a good one? (Laughs.) It was one
o'clock in the morning. A phone call came in. I
worked the night shift. And I said "Holiday Inn." I
said it because we're not Holiday Inn. I was just
70 fooling around. So the boss called me in. She said
"Why did you do it?" I said "Just for a lark. It was
quiet. Nothing to do." She said "Fran, you're a
good operator and we all love you, but I don't know
why you did it." I said "I wanted to have a little
75 fun."

We're supposed to wear our names. Mine's
just Frances. It's not even Frances—I'm Fran. The
assistant manager, we refer to him as mister. I've
always respected a name. These young kids today
80 don't. They call people by their first names. The
last place I worked, we called him mister. He was a
buyer and I figured he should have respect. I'm
only a switchboard operator. I'm Fran. It wouldn't
be miss.

85 But I feel they need us badly. They need us to
be polite and they need us to be nice. You cannot
have a business and have a bad switchboard
operator. We are the hub of that hotel.

And we don't get respect. We don't get it from
90 the bosses or the guests, although they are nice to
us. But if they knew how hard we worked. Today,
communications is the big thing. So much business
is over the phone. I really think we demand a little
more respect.

95 We sit there and we joke "Wouldn't it be great
if we could just take this handful of plugs and just
yank 'em?" (laughs.) We think of it, we think of it.
Like I said, you get so tense . . . If we could just
pull 'em. (Laughs.) Disconnect them and see what
100 happens. You accidentally disconnect somebody,
which happens quite often. You don't do it on
purpose, although there are times when you feel
you'd like to do it.

5.　READING STRATEGY: Getting the meaning from context and from the word itself. Besides the context, sometimes there are clues within a word to help you understand what it means. In the following items consider the meanings of the related words as well as the context. Then circle your answers.

1.　You know the meaning of *across*. *Criss-cross* (line 7) probably means
　　a.　live in.
　　b.　read about.
　　c.　travel around.
2.　You know the meanings of *happy* and *lucky*. *Happy-go-lucky* (line 20) probably means
　　a.　old and tired.
　　b.　careful and serious.
　　c.　relaxed and not worried.
3.　You know the meaning of *frequently*. *Frequented by* (line 22) probably means
　　a.　sometimes used by.
　　b.　often used by.
　　c.　usually owned by.

6.　READING STRATEGY: Using the dictionary. Decide which dictionary definition fits the meaning of the word in the selection.

1.　Which meaning does *mood* have in line 14?

　　mood　*n*　1 in grammar, the aspect of verbs that has to do with the speaker's attitude toward the action or state expressed　2 a feeling or state of mind　3 (plural) periods of bad or changeable feelings

2.　These expressions are listed in the dictionary after the definition of *have*. Which expression has the same meaning as *he had it* in line 54?

　　1 **to have it** (also, **to have got it**)　to understand, to be able to do　2 **to have it** (**with**)　to be tired of, to want to stop or leave　3 **to have it in for**　to be angry and want revenge on　4 **to have on**　to be wearing　5 **to have it out** (**with**)　to discuss, argue or physically fight about a disagreement

3.　Which meaning does *lark* have in line 71?

　　lark　*n*　1 a small songbird of the family Alaudidæ　2 fun, a prank, a good time

4.　Which meaning does *figure* have in line 82?

　　figure　*v*　1 to be conspicuous, in plain sight　2 to make plans　3 to do arithmetic　4 to believe　5 to expect

7.　READING STRATEGY: Inferring and finding specific information. Answer *true* or *false* and discuss why you answered as you did.

1.　Frances Swenson is a real person and lines 25–103 are her own words.　　**T**　F

2.　Frances Swenson considers herself a good worker and a polite, respectable person.　　**T**　F

3.　She thinks everyone should be called by his or her first name.　　T　**F**

4.　She is sorry about saying "Holiday Inn."　　T　**F**

Was Mac mad when Maria got there? What does Larry do that drives Mac crazy?

By seven thirty Maria was glad to leave the hotel. It had been a long day and she was tired. She hurried to the restaurant, where she found Mac waiting for her.

"Hi," she said as she sat down across from him.

Mac looked annoyed. "What happened? I was getting worried."

Maria looked surprised. "Oh, I'm sorry. Didn't you get my message?"

"What message?"

"I called to tell you I'd be late, and Larry promised to leave a note on your desk. Didn't you see it?"

"No, I was late so I didn't go home. I came straight from school."

"Oh, Mac, I'm sorry. They asked me to work late tonight and I didn't want to say no again. I didn't mean to worry you."

"Well, never mind. Let's order. I'm hungry."

Maria looked at her menu, but she kept thinking about her conversation with Larry. "You know, Larry was really rude when I called."

"Was he? I'm not surprised," said Mac. "He usually is. He's really been getting on my nerves."

"What do you mean?"

"Oh, he's such a slob—and he's so inconsiderate. He never cleans or does the dishes and he's always got the radio on when I want to study."

"That'd drive me crazy too," said Maria. "I suppose you've already tried talking to him."

"Yeah, a couple of times, but it didn't do any good."

"Have you thought about asking him to leave?"

"Come on," said Mac impatiently. "You know I can't afford the rent alone. . . . I'll just have to put up with him until school's over."

8. CONVERSATION. Explain why you're late and say that you left a message for your partner.

A: What happened? I was getting worried.
B: Oh, I'm sorry. Didn't you get my message?
A: What message?
B: I called to tell you ...., and .... promised to *tell you/leave you a note*. Didn't you see *him/her/it*?
A: No, ...

> *You can say:*
>
> I called to tell you { I'd be late.
>   I had to work overtime.
>   I couldn't get here on time.

9. CONVERSATION. Complain about someone.

A: ....'s really been getting on my nerves.
B: What do you mean?
A: Oh, *he's/she's so* ..../*such a* .... *(Say what he/she does.)*
B: That'd drive me crazy too. *(Suggest something A can do about the problem.)*
A: Yes, but it didn't do any good. I guess I'll just have to put up with it.   OR   No, but it might be worth a try.

> *You can make a suggestion like this:*
>
> I suppose you've already told her how you feel.
> Have you tried saying no?
> Have you thought about asking him to leave?
> Have you talked to her about it?

> *Here are some ways to complain about people:*
>
> He's such { a slob. He never cleans.
>   a bore. He's always talking about himself.
>   a pain. Every time I turn on the radio, he says he's studying.
>
> She's so { inconsiderate. She's always got the radio on when I want to study.
>   negative. She never says anything nice about anybody or anything.
>   cheap. She never pays for anything.
>   obnoxious. She's rude, she talks too much and she never has a nice thing to say about anybody.

10. WRITING SKILLS. Plan and write a paragraph complaining about someone. It should be similar to the second paragraph of Larry's letter.

A plan of Larry's second paragraph would look like this:

> 1. Mac – a pain
> 2. radio and TV
>   studies all the time
>   cleaning up
> 3. gets on my nerves

To plan your paragraph:

1. Write the person's name and think of a word that describes the person—rude, a slob, inconsiderate, etc. Use this information in the first sentence of your paragraph.

2. Write down a few things that show what you mean—things that the person does. Use these ideas in the middle part of your paragraph.

3. Write down how the person makes you feel. Use this in your last sentence.

This is a letter that Larry wrote to his girlfriend in Philadelphia.

> Dear Sally,
>
> I really miss you, honey. I felt so bad when I called last night and your mother said you were in Norristown. I was looking forward to talking to you so much. On top of that, as soon as I hung up, Mac came home and started bothering me.
>
> He's such a pain. Every time I turn on the radio or the TV, he says he's studying. Of course, that figures -- he never does anything else. I don't know how he can live like that. And he's always nagging me about the dishes and the ashtrays and cleaning the bathtub. He's so unreasonable. He seems to think you have to wash everything right after you use it, and you know I'm not like that. He's really getting on my nerves.
>
> But Mac's only one of my problems. My biggest problem is that I miss you all the time. I'm really counting the days until exams are over and I can come home again.
>
> Well, I've got to go. Lots of love and a big kiss.
>
> XXXX
>
> *Larry*

REVIEW

YOU'VE LEARNED TO

make a request:	Could you do me a favor? Could you stay until nine tonight?
refuse a request, but offer to do something else to help:	Gee, I'm sorry I can't. But I might be able to stay until seven thirty, if that's any help.
accept the offer:	Yeah, that would help.
refuse the offer:	No, I'm afraid it isn't. But thanks anyway.
ask someone to wait for an answer:	I'll let you know for sure as soon as I make a phone call.
leave a message:	Could you give Mac a message for me? Ask him to bring my umbrella.
express concern:	What happened? I was getting worried.
ask for clarification:	What message?
	What do you mean?
report what happened:	I called to tell you I'd be late. Larry promised to leave you a note.
complain about someone:	Larry's really been getting on my nerves. He's such a slob and he's so inconsiderate.
sympathize:	That'd drive me crazy too.
make a suggestion:	I suppose you've already told him how you feel./Have you tried saying no?/Have you thought about asking him to leave?/Have you talked to him about it?
accept the suggestion:	It might be worth a try.
express resignation:	I guess I'll just have to put up with it.

GRAMMAR

After and As soon as + Clause

I'll let you know { after I talk to my mother.
as soon as I make a phone call. }

Tell/Ask

Tell him (that) I'll be late.
Ask him to bring my umbrella.

Present Perfect

I suppose you've already **told** her how you feel.
Have you **tried** saying no?
Have you **thought** about asking him to leave?
Have you **talked** to her about it?

Such + Noun/So + Adjective

He's **such a slob.**
He's **so inconsiderate.**

USEFUL WORDS AND EXPRESSIONS

clean	note	inconsiderate	for sure
give	pain	negative	get on my nerves
promise	radio	obnoxious	I'll let you know.
put up with	slob	overtime	I really appreciate it.
suppose	umbrella	rude	I was getting worried.
turn on	•	•	It didn't do any good.
wait for	anybody	always	on time
•	anything	such	Thanks a lot.
bore	himself	too much	Thanks anyway.
help	•	•	You're welcome.
message	cheap	Could you do me a favor?	

1. Complete the conversations and say them with a partner.

I. You want Mac to give Maria a message for you.

YOU: When you see Maria, could you ....
.... for me?

MAC: Sure. What is it?

YOU: She promised to ....,
but .... Could you
....?

MAC: OK. I'll tell her as soon as ....
....

YOU: OK, thanks. I really appreciate it. Tell her I'll
call her after ....

MAC: Sure.

II. Now you want Larry Allen to do you a favor.

YOU: Hey, Larry. Could you ....
....?

LARRY: Maybe. What do you want?

YOU: ....

LARRY: Hmm. Look, I'm kind of busy. I might be able
to ...., if that's any help.

YOU: Uh, well, no, I'm afraid ....
...., but thanks anyway.

LARRY: Yeah, sure.

2. Maria is at work. She is talking to Mr. Pushkin, the general manager of the Regency. Circle the right verb and fill in the blanks with *to* if it's needed.

MARIA: Mr. Pushkin, Miss Taft just called .... *leave/let* you know about the
$\underset{1}{}$ $\underset{2}{}$
next managers' meeting.

MR. PUSHKIN: Oh, yes. Did she *leave/let* a message for me?
$\underset{3}{}$

MARIA: No, she just *said/told* it's going .... be at 9:00 A.M on the 18th.
$\underset{4}{}$ $\underset{5}{}$

MR. PUSHKIN: Fine. . . . Oh, could you please .... *call/say* .... Mr. Jenkins and *say/tell*
$\underset{6}{}$ $\underset{7}{}$ $\underset{8}{}$ $\underset{9}{}$
.... him about the meeting too? *Ask/Say* .... him .... make a note of it
$\underset{10}{}$ $\underset{11}{}$ $\underset{12}{}$ $\underset{13}{}$
on his calendar. Then come back here. I've got .... *say/talk* .... you
$\underset{14}{}$ $\underset{15}{}$ $\underset{16}{}$
about some new guest registration procedures.

3. CONVERSATION

A:

B just arrived at your house. You've been waiting for him/her because you're going out together. B's late.

Say you were getting worried:
Hey, ...

Say you didn't get the message and ask B what happened.

Sympathize and give advice:
.... *I suppose you've already* ....?

B:

You just arrived at A's house. You and A are going out and you're late.

You called A's house earlier. A wasn't home, so you left a message saying you'd be late:
Didn't ....? *I called to tell you* ....

Tell A you had a problem with someone at school/ work and describe the person:
.... *He's/She's so/such* .... *He's/ She's really been getting on my nerves.*

Answer:
Yes, but .... *I guess I'll just* ....

UNIT 8 I thought we were going out.

What did Maria and Mac fight about? Whose fault was it?

One Sunday afternoon Maria met Mac in Central Park. They planned to study for a while and then go get something to eat. Maria hoped they would have time to see a movie too.

By four o'clock she had finished all the work she'd brought with her and was getting bored. She started a letter to a friend, but soon she put it aside.

"Mac," she said, "I'm getting hungry. How much longer are you going to be?"

"Oh, an hour, an hour and a half."

"An hour and a half! By then it'll be too late to go to a movie or anything."

"I'm sorry, but I can't stop until I finish going over my notes."

"Well, I wish you'd told me you were going to study all day. I thought we were going out."

"Come on, Maria. You knew I had to study. I told you I had a test tomorrow."

"Yeah, but you didn't tell me it was going to take you so long. If I'd known, I would've made plans to do something else."

"Well, don't let me keep you," said Mac sarcastically. "It wasn't *my* idea to study together anyway."

"I see. All right, if that's the way you feel about it . . ." Maria stood up and picked up her books.

Mac already regretted the way he'd talked to her. "I'll call you later," he said.

"Yeah," she said coldly.

He watched unhappily as she walked away.

1. CONVERSATION

A: You're waiting for **B** and you're getting impatient.

A: .... How much longer are you going to be?
B: ....
A: ....! (*By then it'll be too late to* ....)
B: I'm sorry, but I can't *stop/leave* until ....

B: You aren't ready to leave yet.

You can say:

I'm getting hungry.
It's getting late. } How much longer are
It's almost four o'clock. } you going to be?

You can say:

I can't *stop/leave* until { I finish going over my notes.
my parents call.
my boss does.

2. CONVERSATION

A: You're still waiting for **B** and now you're annoyed.

A: I wish you'd told me .... I thought ....

B: Come on. You knew .... OR I told you ....

A: Yeah, but you didn't tell me .... If I'd known, I *would've/wouldn't have* ....

B: You thought **A** understood that you were going to be delayed.

You can say:

I wish you'd told me you **were going to study** all day.
I thought we **had** a date.
You knew I **couldn't go** out.
I told you I **had to study**.
You didn't tell me it **was going to take** so long.

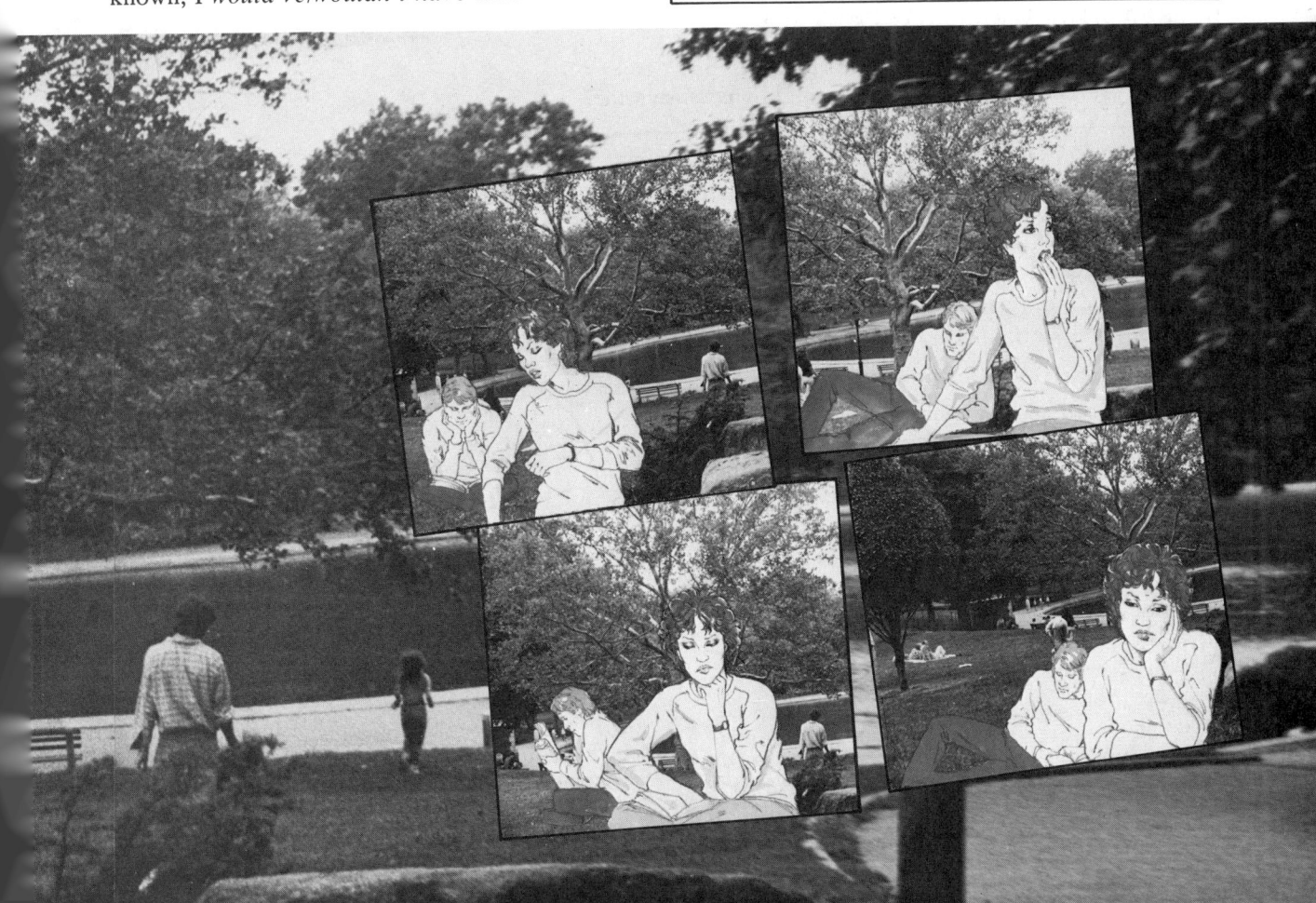

3.   GRAMMAR FOCUS. Here's the letter Maria started writing while she was waiting for Mac. Fill in the blanks with the right form of the verbs.

Dear Terry,

I'm sitting in the park keeping Mac company while he studies and I'm quietly going crazy. Since he started studying for exams, he doesn't seem to have time to do anything else. If I'd known it was going to be like this, I _____ (1. suggest) studying together this afternoon. We were going to study for a while and then go to a movie or something. Well, it's been four hours and he hasn't even mentioned stopping. If he'd told me he was going to study so long, I _____ (2. make) other plans.
(To be continued.)

4.   READING STRATEGY: Predicting.

1.   This is the title of an article that appeared in *U.S. News and World Report*, a weekly newsmagazine.

Interview With Angus Campbell,
Professor of Psychology and Sociology, University of Michigan

The Happiest Americans—Who They Are

The article will probably:

a. tell you about the happiest family in the United States.
b. give a list of names and addresses of the happiest people in the United States.
c. tell which kinds (or groups) of Americans are the happiest.
     Explain why you answered as you did.

2.   This paragraph appeared after the title and before the interview. Do you still think you answered No. 1 correctly? Explain why or why not.

People are less joyous these days than in the carefree 1950s, a survey shows—but why do the elderly seem to be happier than young adults? A survey official tells of the findings, and what they suggest.

5.   READING STRATEGIES: Finding specific information and note-taking. As you read the article on the next page, look for the answers to these questions. When you find an answer, write down a few words (not complete sentences) to help you remember it.

1.   Why are young people less happy today than in the 1950s?
2.   Why are older people happier than young people?
3.   Some young people are happier than others. Why?

Reprinted from "U.S. News & World Report"

Interview With Angus Campbell,
Professor of Psychology and Sociology, University of Michigan

The Happiest Americans—Who They Are

People are less joyous these days than in the carefree 1950s, a survey shows—but why do the elderly seem to be happier than young adults? A survey official tells of the findings, and what they suggest.

Q. Professor Campbell, are Americans as happy and contented with their lot as they were 20 years ago?

A. No. Our surveys since 1957 show a clear deterioration in people's feelings of well-being and happiness with life. The trend reached a low point in 1972 and had recovered only modestly in our most recent survey last year.

Q. Why has there been this overall decline, especially among young people who have had many advantages and have so much of their lives still ahead of them?

A. It's largely an expression of the major traumas of the '60s and '70s—Vietnam, racial confrontation, urban insurrection, Watergate, economic stress.

Vietnam must have been a very damaging factor. In 1957 young adults were busy "making it"— getting married, having babies, riding the economic boom upward. The generation that followed was selected by an unkind fate to fight an unpopular war, and it is not surprising that its feelings of well-being are more negative.

The interesting thing is that the dampening effect has continued through succeeding years. Despite the fact that Vietnam is receding into history, the cloud that depressed young people in the late 1960s does not appear to have lifted.

What is also true is that the young, the affluent and the better educated are more sensitive to the implications of current events. They tend to lead opinion change in many areas of modern life— women's liberation, civil rights, conservation, consumer protest—and their feelings of well-being may be more responsive to political and economic trends than those of the rest of the population.

Q. Does marriage seem to affect the "happiness quotient"?

A. Not only is marriage influential; it is the key determinant of happiness among young adults.

About half of the 18–to–30 age group are unmarried. Those young singles, both men and women, are the most negative in their outlook toward life. Despite the fact that they have had recent positive experiences—feeling excited, proud, pleased, on top of the world—they also report being restless, lonely, bored, depressed and upset. The exuberance of youth that we might expect to find in these young unmarried people seems strangely absent.

Marriage changes that picture to a remarkable degree. The presence of a spouse enhances a person's happiness more than any other single factor.

Our surveys confirm again and again that the marital relationship is the basic source of social support among adult Americans—the single most important contributor to a person's sense of well-being.

Q. Why is the feeling of satisfaction so high among older persons generally?

A. I think it's because they are more settled, less eager for new experiences and simply satisfied with less. They have come to terms with life and learned to live with reality. They know what they can expect and what they cannot expect. A younger person, who doesn't have that kind of experience, starts out with aspirations and hopes and expectations that may turn out to be quite unrealistic.

Older people may also be more carefree because of better Social Security and pension and medical benefits, and also because of the various community projects and housing programs that have been set up for older persons and retirees.

Q. How would you describe the typical "happy American"?

A. It would be different for men and women. For a woman, she is an individual under 30, who is married and does not yet have a child. It wouldn't matter whether she was working or not, but she would be in average or better economic circumstances. It is fair to say that women in this situation are living a euphoric existence compared to most other women.

The man is between 50 and 70, married and living with his wife at home after the children have grown and moved away.

6.   WRITING SKILLS. Read the first sentence of the letter about "The Happiest Americans." The sentence gives the main idea of the letter. Some of the sentences in the box below support this main idea. Complete the letter. Don't change the order of the sentences.

I was truly surprised to read that marriage "is the key determinant of happiness among young adults." ...

> As a marriage counselor, I have worked with hundreds of young couples who are having trouble staying together.
>
> However, I have an uncle who has been very happily married for almost 50 years. He and his wife live in Florida now.
>
> Many of these people have been married for less than a year and are already thinking of a divorce.
>
> I can assure you that *they* would not agree with the article.
>
> It is difficult to say whether having children helps a marriage or not.
>
> To them marriage has come to mean only trouble and frustration.
>
> Sharing is also an important part of marriage.
>
> When everything works out, marriage certainly does make young people feel happier.

Where has Franco been?
How do Maria and Franco know each other?
Is Franco going to be in New York very long?

When Maria left Mac in the park, she was upset about their fight. She was walking down the street with her head down, deep in thought, when suddenly she heard someone call her name.

FRANCO: Hey, Maria!

MARIA: Franco! I haven't seen you for ages. Where've you been?

FRANCO: In Florida. I just got back a couple of days ago. Hey, it's great to see you. You look terrific. I like your hair that way.

MARIA: Thanks. You're looking good yourself.

FRANCO: Are you going this way? I'll walk with you. Here, let me carry those books for you. So what've you been up to? Are you still studying English?

MARIA: No, not this semester. I don't have time.

FRANCO: How about the people from our class? Do you ever see any of them?

MARIA: Yeah, I see Tomiko a lot. And Tony writes once in a while.

FRANCO: Oh, yeah? How is he?

MARIA: He's fine. He's running his family's restaurant now.

FRANCO: That's terrific. I bet he's good at it. What about the others? What ever happened to that tall African woman who looked like a model?

MARIA: Oh, you mean Jeannette Kaba?

FRANCO: Yeah. Is she still around?

MARIA: I don't know. I haven't seen her since the course was over. She and her husband were talking about going back to the Ivory Coast, though.

FRANCO: Gee, it's great to see you ...

MARIA: It's nice to see you too. So what are you going to do now? Are you going to register at NYU again?

FRANCO: No. I'm going to stay in New York for a little while and then I'm going back to Italy.

7. CONVERSATION. Ask about someone whose name you don't remember.

A: What ever happened to that .... who
    ....?

B: Oh, you mean ....? OR Oh, yeah. I know
    who you mean, but I don't remember *his/her* name.

A: (*Yeah.*) Is *he/she* still ....-ing ..../*still
    around?*

B: I don't know. I haven't seen *him/her since/for*
    .... OR   Yeah, (*I think*) *he/she* ....

Here are some ways to describe what people look like:		
that { tall / short / heavyset / thin	{ good-looking / attractive / interesting-looking	man/woman/ girl/boy/guy

There are more descriptive words on page 15.

Here are some ways to describe the way people act:

smart	boring	quiet
funny	shy	loud

And you can also give additional information about people like this:

What ever happened to that man/woman . . .

. . . who { looked like a model. / was always sleeping in class. / never got to work on time. / used to bring his kids to the office.

8. GRAMMAR FOCUS. Fill in the blanks as in the example, using *who* and the words indicated.

FRANCO: Oh, hey. Remember that shy guy ..... *who*
         always sat in the back row?
         1. always sit in the back row

MARIA: You mean Oscar? The one ....
         2. bring
         ....
         wine and cheese for everybody
         just before Christmas?

FRANCO: I don't remember that. I guess I was

         absent. He was the one ....
         3. always
         .... He always wore a dark suit
         look like a banker
         and tie—very conservative.

MARIA: Right. That's Oscar. What about him?

FRANCO: Well, the other day I saw him wearing jeans and
         a leather jacket and riding a motorcycle.

MARIA: No! Are you sure it was Oscar?

FRANCO: Yeah. He waved at me. And there was a girl

         with him ....
         4. look like a model
         —I mean, really attractive.

9. 🎞 **LISTENING. Maria and Franco are still discussing their former classmates. Listen to their conversation and answer the questions.**

1. Do they remember the name of the person Franco is talking about?
2. What did he look like?

10. **CONVERSATION. Tony Costa and Tomiko Sato are friends of yours. They used to go out together when they both lived in New York. Tomiko still lives in New York, but Tony had to go back to Brazil.**

A: Read the letter you just got from Tony and practice the conversation below.	**B:** Read the letter you just got from Tomiko and practice the conversation below.

Dear A,

   Sorry I haven't written for so long. I got sick in January and I couldn't go to the restaurant for three weeks. I'm OK now, but there were some problems at the restaurant while I was out and I had to fire the cook. Now I have to do a lot of the cooking myself until I can find a replacement. I've just about given up on the idea of going back to school. I'm too busy at the restaurant. I don't think I'll even be able to take a vacation this year.
   Well, look, take care of yourself and say hi to everybody for me.
   And write!

                    Tony

Dear B,

   I've got a free minute at work, so I thought I'd write a short note to let you know why I haven't written. It's mainly because I've been so busy lately. I'm working full time at Japan Air Lines now and I'm still taking English at NYU.
   Besides, I've been going out practically every night. Takeo's smart and very nice and we have a lot of the same interests, but he still hasn't made me forget Tony. I know I should forget him -- I'll probably never see him again -- but I can't.
   Anyway, right now I've got to get back to my desk, but I promise to write you a longer letter soon.

                    Love,
                    Tomiko

A/B:	Do you ever hear from *Tomiko/Tony?*
B/A:	Yeah. I got a letter from *him/her* last ....
A/B:	Oh, yeah? How is *he/she?*
B/A:	*He's/She's* fine (*but*) ....
A AND B:	Continue the conversation. Use the information in the letter you read.

REVIEW

YOU'VE LEARNED TO

express impatience:	I'm getting hungry. How much longer are you going to be? Oh, an hour and a half. An hour and a half! By then it'll be too late to go to a movie or anything.
apologize and explain:	I'm sorry, but I can't stop until I finish going over my notes.
complain to someone about his/her behavior:	I wish you'd told me you were going to study all day. I thought we were going out.
defend yourself:	Come on. You knew I had to study.
say what you would have done, but didn't do:	If I'd known, I would've made plans to do something else.
talk about someone you used to know:	Do you ever hear from Tony? Yeah. I got a letter from him last week. He's fine. He's running his family's restaurant now. What ever happened to that tall African woman who looked like a model? Is she still around? I don't know. I haven't seen her since the course was over.
ask for confirmation:	You mean Jeannette Kaba?

GRAMMAR

Until + Clause

I can't leave **until I finish going over my notes.**

If Clause: Past Unreal Conditional

If I'd known, { I wouldn't **have waited.**
I **would've made** other plans.

Relative Clause: Who

What ever happened to that tall African woman **who looked like a model?**

Wish + Past Perfect

I **wish** you'd **(had) told** me (that) you were going to study all day.

For/Since with Present Perfect

I **haven't seen** him { **since** the course was over.
since January.
for six months.

USEFUL WORDS AND EXPRESSIONS

go out	date	funny	almost
go over	kid	heavyset	ever
hear from	model	impatient	•
knew (know)	parent	loud	by then
known (know)	person	quiet	How much longer?
•	•	shy	what ever happened to
boss	attractive	smart	
		•	

1. Fill in the blanks with the correct words.

I. Joyce Elbert, a friend of Maria's, is coming to New York on business. She is calling Maria, who is planning to meet her at the airport.

MARIA: Hello?

JOYCE: Maria! I'm glad you're home. I've been trying to

get you .... half an hour.
        1. for/since

MARIA: Where are you?

JOYCE: I'm .... in Montreal. There's
      2. ever/still

something wrong with the plane and we

.... leave ....
   3. can't/aren't   4. until/
.... they fix it. So far nobody seems to
as soon as
know how much ....
        5. later/longer
it ....
     6. 's going to take/takes

MARIA: Oh, no!

JOYCE: Yeah. So look, don't bother to meet me at the airport, OK? By the time I get there,

it .... too late .... do
   7. 's/'ll be   8. to/for
anything tonight. I .... to the
        9. 'll go/go
hotel and call you in the morning.

MARIA: OK, I'll talk to you then. Bye.

II. It's Saturday and Mac's roommate, Larry, is about to leave the apartment.

LARRY: OK. I'm off for the weekend. See you Monday.

MAC: Hey, I thought we ....
        1. 're going to/were going to
work on your car today.

LARRY: Oh. I .... all about that. Well,
     2. forgot/forget
thanks anyway, but I ....
         3. won't be able to/can
do it today.

MAC: Well, I wish you .... me you
        4. told/'d told
.... me. If I ....
   5. 'd need/didn't need   6. know/
....................., I ....
'd known   7. 'd made/would've made
other plans.

LARRY: Sorry. I thought I .... you. . . .
        8. tell/told
Well, I'll see you.

MAC: Yeah.

2.   CONVERSATION

A:

> You and **B** planned to have dinner together. You are waiting for **B** at the restaurant. A waiter has just called you to the telephone.

B:

> You and **A** planned to have dinner together at a restaurant. However, you're delayed at work. Call **A** at the restaurant.

> Answer the phone.

> Ask why.

> Find out when **B** is going to get there:
> *Oh. . . . Well, how much longer* ....?

> Accept **B**'s apology and say you'll wait for him/her.

> Identify yourself and tell **A** you're going to be late:
> .... *I'm sorry, but* ....

> Explain:
> .... *and I can't leave until* ....

> Answer. Then apologize again:
> .... *I'm really sorry. If I'd known,*
> ....

> End the conversation.

3.   Two friends are running in the park after work. Complete the conversation and say it with a partner.

FIRST FRIEND: Guess who I saw on the way to work this morning.

SECOND FRIEND: Who?

FIRST FRIEND: Johnny Sanderson.

SECOND FRIEND: Johnny Sanderson! I .... him for ....

FIRST FRIEND: Yeah, that's because he .... since .... He got back .... ago.

SECOND FRIEND: He and I ran in the Interstate Marathon together. If .... I ....asked him to run with us. What's he doing these days anyway?

.... still ....

........................?

FIRST FRIEND: No, he quit. Now .... As a matter of fact, he says he has to travel a lot. He's just here for a few days between trips.

SECOND FRIEND: Oh, yeah? .... is he going to be in town?

FIRST FRIEND: Probably about a week.

SECOND FRIEND: Then where's he going?

FIRST FRIEND: He told me .... to Paris next, but he can't leave until ....

THE ADVENTURE CONTINUES

The three outlaws from Krypton descend to Earth to confront the Man of Steel, in a cosmic battle for world supremacy.

SUPERMAN II

ALEXANDER SALKIND presents GENE HACKMAN · CHRISTOPHER REEVE

"SUPERMAN II"

NED BEATTY · JACKIE COOPER · SARAH DOUGLAS

SUSANNAH YORK   CLIFTON JAMES · and E.G. MARSHALL as The President · MARC McCLURE

MARGOT KIDDER · JACK O'HALLORAN · VALERIE PERRINE · SUSANNAH YORK   Story by MARIO PUZO   Screenplay by MARIO PUZO

and TERENCE STAMP   PANAVISION® TECHNICOLOR®   DOLBY STEREO™ IN SELECTED THEATRES

Production Design JOHN BARRY   Music Composed and Conducted by KEN THORNE   From Original Material Composed by JOHN WILLIAMS   Creative Consultant TOM MANKIEWICZ   Directed by RICHARD LESTER   An ALEXANDER and ILYA SALKIND Production

DAVID NEWMAN and LESLIE NEWMAN   Executive Producer ILYA SALKIND   Produced by PIERRE SPENGLER

Original Sound Track Available on Warner Bros. Records & Tapes.

Distributed by Warner Bros.
A Warner Communications Company

© DC COMICS Inc. 1981
All Rights Reserved.

PG PARENTAL GUIDANCE SUGGESTED
SOME MATERIAL MAY NOT BE SUITABLE FOR CHILDREN

What didn't Maria like about the movie?
Why didn't she like that part?
What did Franco like about the movie?

The day after they ran into each other, Maria and Franco went to see *Superman II*. They were discussing the movie as they came out of the theater.

"That was a good movie, wasn't it?" said Franco.

"Yeah, it was. Actually, the only thing I didn't like was when those three outlaws destroyed that small town. It was so violent."

"Yeah," said Franco, "that was pretty bad. But the rest of the movie was fun. I thought the best part was when Lois Lane found out Clark Kent was Superman."

"Yeah, but wasn't it sad when he gave up his powers so he could marry her and have a normal life?"

"Oh, come on," said Franco, smiling. "That was true love.

Maria laughed. "Rossetti, you're such a romantic."

"Of course, but that's the secret of my charm."

"You and Clark Kent would make a good team," said Maria as she took Franco's arm. "But, seriously, wasn't Christopher Reeve good?"

"Yeah, he was pretty good."

"And he's so handsome."

"Did you see him in *Somewhere in Time?*"

"No, I never saw it."

"I didn't think he was as good in that. He played this writer who fell in love with a woman who lived a long time ago. It was sort of weird. . . . Anyway, what do you want to do now?"

1.   CONVERSATION. Decide on a movie that both of you have seen. Talk about specific parts that you liked or didn't like.

A: .... was a *good/fantastic/really interesting* movie, wasn't it?

B: Yeah, it was. I thought the .... part was when ....

A: Yeah, *and/but* wasn't it .... when .... ?

B/A: Actually, the only thing I didn't like was *when/that* ....

You can say:

A: That was a **good** movie, wasn't it?
B: Yeah, it was. I thought the **best** part was . . .

You can also say that movies (or parts of them) were:

funny	scary	romantic
sad	exciting	powerful, etc.

You can talk about parts of a movie like this:

I thought { the best part was when Lois Lane found out Clark Kent was Superman.

the funniest part was when Clark Kent was trying to fight that guy in the restaurant.

The only thing I didn't like was when those three outlaws destroyed that small town.

2. GRAMMAR FOCUS. Fill in the blanks with one item from I and one item from II. Use all of the items.

I	II
that I	changed drivers
when you	went to Florida
when they	started smoking a cigar
when somebody	met some interesting people

MARIA: Tell me about ....
                                        1
....

Did you go alone?

FRANCO: Uh-huh.

MARIA: How'd you get there?

FRANCO: On the bus. It wasn't very comfortable, but I saw a lot more of the country. The

best thing was ....
                                        2
....

MARIA: Where'd you stop on the way? Did you see Washington?

FRANCO: No, I took an express and we never left

the highway except ....
                                        3
....

MARIA: It must have been a long trip.

FRANCO: Almost 28 hours, but it wasn't bad. There was only one time I wished I'd taken the

plane. That was ....
                                        4
....

I thought I was going to be sick.

3. CONVERSATION. Compare an actor or actress' performance in two different movies.

A: Wasn't .... good (*in* ....)?

B: Yeah, and *he's/she's so/such* ....

A: Did you see *him/her* in .... ?

B: No, I never saw it.   OR   Yeah.

A: *I didn't think he/she was as good in that. He/She* played this .... who ....

B/A: (Continue the conversation.)

> *If the movie's playing in your town right now, you can say:*
>
> Have you seen *Somewhere in Time?*
> No, not yet.

From the motion picture "SOMEWHERE IN TIME" Courtesy of Universal Pictures (Universal, 1980)

Somewhere in Time

Superman and Lois Lane are trademarks of DC Comics Inc. and are used with permission. Copyright © 1980 DC Comics Inc.

Superman II

Where does Maria want to go?
Who's going with her?
What's there to do in and around Fort Lauderdale?

After the movie Franco and Maria decided to take a walk. It was a warm night, so they stopped to get an ice cream cone.

"You were really lucky to be able to go to Florida," said Maria. "I haven't been out of New York since before Christmas and that was only for four days."

"Are you going anywhere for vacation this year?"

"Yeah. Tomiko and I thought we'd go somewhere together."

"Oh, yeah? Where are you going?"

"We haven't decided yet, but I want to go someplace with lots of sun, where we can swim and play tennis."

"Listen, if that's what you're looking for, you should go to Fort Lauderdale."

"Won't it be too hot by then?"

"I don't think so. And you might get off-season rates."

Maria looked interested. "What's there to do besides lie on the beach?"

"Lots. There are a lot of places to eat, dance, meet people. It's full of students."

"Sounds good. Are there any tours worth taking?"

"I suppose so. I think they've got trips to the Keys—you know, the islands south of Florida. And you can always go to Miami. If you go at night, be sure to go to Dino's. They've got fantastic Cuban music."

"That sounds like exactly the kind of vacation I'm looking for."

"Oh, you'll have a good time."

4. CONVERSATION

A:

> Ask about **B**'s vacation plans:
> *Where are you going (for)* ....?

> Suggest a place you've been to:
> *Listen, if that's what you're looking for, you should go to* ....

> Respond to **B**'s objection.

> Answer and make a suggestion:
> *You can* .... *If* ...., *be sure to* ....

B:

> Respond:
> *I haven't decided yet, but I want to go someplace with/where* ....

> Object to **A**'s suggestion:
> *Won't it/there be* ....? OR *Isn't it* ....? OR *Isn't/Aren't there* ....?

> Ask for more information:
> *What's there to do besides* ....? OR
> *Are there any* {
>   *tours worth taking?*
>   *restaurants worth trying?*
>   *nightclubs worth going to?*
>   *museums worth visiting?*
> }
> OR
> *Is there anything worth buying?*

5.   FOLLOW-UP. Here's part of an article from the travel section of the *New York News*. Complete the article with information about a place you've been to.

Looking for someplace with/where ....? You should go to .... There are .... and the .... is/are really worth .... If you go, be sure to .... It's ....

6. LISTENING. Listen while Franco gives Maria information about where to stay in Fort Lauderdale. Take notes. Write down the <u>name</u> of the place Franco recommends and the <u>cost per night.</u> You can also write down anything else you would want to remember.

Pier Hotel — 24 / double
toilet, — 4 blocks to the beach

7. APPLYING READING STRATEGIES: Read the brochure. Then discuss your choice for the Holiday Jubilee Sweepstakes and fill out the coupon.

Here's how you and your companion can be Grand Prizewinners in the Holiday Jubilee Sweepstakes:

1. Decide which holiday you and your companion would like to win.
2. Fill in the coupon with your name, address and the name of your companion, and check the holiday you want to take.
3. Send the coupon to HOLIDAY JUBILEE SWEEPSTAKES, Box 1980, Kalamazoo, Michigan 49003.

HOLIDAY JUBILEE SWEEPSTAKES

NAME _____

ADDRESS _____
STREET _____ STATE _____ ZIP
CITY

NAME OF YOUR COMPANION _____

☐ **HOLIDAY 1** New York City **BROADWAY EXTRAVAGANZA**

☐ **HOLIDAY 2** New Orleans **MARDI GRAS MAGIC**

☐ **HOLIDAY 3** Las Vegas **THE 24-HOUR CITY**

☐ **HOLIDAY 4** Grand Canyon Raft Trip **WILDERNESS ADVENTURE**

☐ **HOLIDAY 5** Washington, D.C. **LIVING HISTORY**

☐ **HOLIDAY 6** Hollywood/Disneyland **STARDUST ENCHANTMENT**

Employees of the Holiday Jubilee Co. and their immediate families not eligible.

HOLIDAY 1 New York City **BROADWAY EXTRAVAGANZA**

- Six nights at the elegant Waldorf-Astoria Hotel
- Your choice of Broadway shows, theater, music and dance.
- Art museums and galleries.
- All the world-famous sights of New York—the Empire State Building, the World Trade Center, the Statue of Liberty, Times Square and Broadway, Greenwich Village, the United Nations, Chinatown, the Stock Exchange.
- Plus special sightseeing tours designed for you—New York architecture, fashion, sports. You name it!

HOLIDAY 2 New Orleans **MARDI GRAS MAGIC** Feb. 5 – Feb. 19 only

- Five nights at the Royal Sonesta Hotel.
- First-class seats for all the Mardi Gras Parades.
- Dance all night at one of the Krewe Balls, the masked costume balls given by the clubs which organize the Mardi Gras carnival celebration.
- A tour of the top jazz halls to hear the authentic sound of New Orleans.
- Visits to plantations outside the city.
- An overnight Mississippi riverboat trip on the "Southern Belle."

8. WRITING SKILLS. You're planning to visit a place in the United States. Write a letter to the Chamber of Commerce of the city or state you want to visit and ask for the information you need.

For information about a city, write:

    Chamber of Commerce
    (City), (State) (ZIP Code, if known)
    U.S.A.

For information about a state, write:

    Chamber of Commerce
    (Capital City), (State) (ZIP Code, if known)
    U.S.A.

1. In the first paragraph of your letter, say when you're going and how long you plan to stay.

2. In the second paragraph, you should say exactly what you want to see and do and ask for specific information (inexpensive hotels near Disneyland, how to get tickets for Broadway plays, etc.).

You can also ask them to send you things like a map of Disneyland or a schedule of White House tours.

3. In your third paragraph, you can ask for information about other things to see and do in the area, based on your interests (tennis courts in Las Vegas, a park where you can go running in New Orleans, places where you can buy books and magazines in your own language in New York, etc.).

HOLIDAY 3   Las Vegas
THE 24-HOUR CITY

- Six nights at the world-famous Caesar's Palace Hotel.
- Choice tables for any shows in town—no restrictions.
- Private lessons in all the games—roulette, baccarat, keno, blackjack—from famed gambler John "Blackjack" Masterson.
- $1,000 in casino chips. Keep your winnings.
- Unlimited use of hotel facilities and of the Sahara Country Club. Swimming, tennis, golf, sauna, massage, and much, much more.

HOLIDAY 4   Grand Canyon Raft Trip
WILDERNESS ADVENTURE

13 days, 225 miles and dozens of rapids on the Colorado, the West's most spectacular river. Absolute peace and quiet punctuated by moments of sheer terror.
Inflated oar-powered boats carry five passengers and a boatman.
Without noisy boat engines, you'll be able to approach big-horn sheep, deer, beaver and other wildlife.
Trips on foot to several waterfalls and side canyons, including beautiful Havasu Canyon, home of the Havasupai Indians.
Experienced guides make your trip safe and informative.
Swimming, fishing, sunbathing, camping, fine outdoor food.

HOLIDAY 5   Washington, D.C.
LIVING HISTORY

- Six nights at the luxurious Four Seasons Hotel
- Choice seats for theater, music and dance at the Kennedy Center for the Performing Arts.
- Tours of all the well-known sights—the Washington Monument, Kennedy Center for the Performing Arts, Lincoln Memorial, Jefferson Memorial, the Capitol, the National Gallery, Georgetown and the White House.
- A special tour of the capital's incomparable museums, designed to suit your interests—history, art, natural history, and science or technology.
- A one-day luxury cruise down the Potomac River on a private yacht to visit Mount Vernon, home of first President George Washington.

HOLIDAY 6   Hollywood/Disneyland
STARDUST ENCHANTMENT

- Six nights at the legendary Beverly Hills Hotel.

Hollywood
- An evening with a famous Hollywood star. Cocktails and dinner at Trader Vic's Polynesian restaurant, a private screening of the star's latest film, dancing and drinks at a famous Hollywood nightclub.
- Do a screen test for a top Hollywood studio. Maybe **you** can be a star!

Disneyland
- Unlimited tickets for Disneyland rides and events. Return as often as you want.
- VIP treatment.

4. Thank them in your fourth paragraph.

Before you begin writing the letter, make notes to *plan* your second and third paragraphs.

REVIEW

**YOU'VE
LEARNED TO**

talk about a movie:	That was a good movie, wasn't it?
	Yeah, it was. I thought the best part was when Lois Lane found out Clark Kent was Superman.
	Yeah, but wasn't it sad when he had to give up his powers so he could marry her?
talk about something you didn't like:	Actually, the only thing I didn't like was when those three outlaws destroyed that small town. It was so violent.
talk about an actor/actress:	Wasn't Christopher Reeve good?
	And he's so handsome.
	He played this writer who fell in love with a woman who lived a long time ago.
compare:	I thought he was even better in *Somewhere in Time.*/I didn't think he was as good in *Somewhere in Time*.
talk about future plans:	Where are you going for vacation?
	We haven't decided yet, but I want to go somewhere with lots of sun.
make a suggestion:	If that's what you're looking for, you should go to Fort Lauderdale.
	You can always go to Miami. If you do, be sure to go to Dino's.
object to the suggestion:	Won't it be too hot by then?
ask for further information:	What's there to do besides lie on the beach? Are there any tours worth taking?

GRAMMAR

Comparatives

> I thought he was even **better** in *Somewhere in Time*.
> I didn't think he was **as good** in *Somewhere in Time*.

Noun Clauses

> The only thing I didn't like was **when the outlaws destroyed that town.**
> I thought the best part was **when Lois Lane found out Clark Kent was Superman.**

Negative Questions

> **Wasn't it** sad when he had to give up his powers so he could marry her?
> **Wasn't Christopher Reeve** good?
> **Won't it be** too hot by then?

USEFUL WORDS AND EXPRESSIONS

destroy	outlaw	romantic	never
fight	part	sad	somewhere
found out (find out)	tour	scary	•
look for	•	those	The only thing I
•	great	•	didn't like . . .
nightclub	powerful	actually	

1. CONVERSATION. You and your partner were both at the same party last night.

A:

Start the conversation:
That was a .... party last night, wasn't it?

Say what *you* liked or didn't like:
Yeah. And wasn't it funny/fun/terrible when ....?

Respond.

B:

Agree, but mention something that was good or bad:
Yeah, it was. The only thing I didn't like/liked was ....

Agree:
Yeah, ...

Continue the conversation.

2. B and someone else are going out to celebrate a birthday, anniversary, promotion, etc. Complete the conversation and say it with a partner.

A: Where are you and .... going to

celebrate ....?

B: .... yet, but ....

.... someplace where/with

....

A: Listen, if ...., you should

....

3. This review was in the *New York News*. Fill in the blanks with the words from the list. Use each word once.

should	the	as	be sure to
besides	what	most	who
decide to	worth	even	when

ON BROADWAY THIS WEEK
by Ed Walters

If a different kind of comedy is ....*what*.... you're
looking for, you really ....*should*.... see Bert Muller's *Supersell* at the Rosebud Theater. Mr. Muller's last play on
Broadway was the very successful *Anytime You Say*. *Supersell*
isn't ....*as*.... funny, but it is a delightful play and
full of surprises. As a matter of fact, it's probably the only
new play ....*worth*.... seeing on Broadway right now.

Perhaps ....*the*.... biggest attraction is an excellent
performance by Mel Fisher. He plays Les Butler, a quiet, shy
salesclerk ....*who*.... becomes a super salesman
....*when*.... he needs to make $50,000 in one week. He is
helped by Gwen Gould (played by Jennifer Karle), a young
woman who is trying to find something to do ....*besides*....
drive her parents crazy. You might remember Karle from
her award-winning role in *The Happy Hour*. She's
....*be sure to*.... ....*even*.... funnier in this play.

Supersell is full of laughs. There is one surprise after another,
right up to the end, which is the ....*most*.... amusing
part of all.

An added attraction: Benny Jackson plays the piano in the
lobby before curtain time and during intermission. So if you
....*decide to*.... see this wonderful play, ...*be sure*....
get there early.

CONSOLIDATION UNIT 10 I've been trying to call you.

HOW CAN I TELL YOU THAT I LOVE YOU?
(IF YOU WON'T ANSWER MY CALL)

Steven Brandick

1. May-be it was wrong to keep you though I had my work to do.
2. May-be I got a wrong num-ber. May-be there's a twist-ed line.
3. May-be your heart's o-ver-crow-ded. May-be mine's beating out of time

I just want-ed you there with me and did-n't no-tice how time flew.
May-be the cir-cuit's o-ver loaded. You know it hap-pens all the time.
May-be there's a wall be-tween us made of hopes and thoughts and sighs

May-be it was wrong to let you walk out on me and all
Talked to all the op-er-a-tors. Said your phone's ringing off the wall.
Si-lence is a dead-ly wea-pon kill-ing love like a cannon ball.

1.3. To Coda

But I can't tell you that I love you if you won't an-swer my call.
And I can't tell you that I love you if you won't an-swer my
And I can't tell you that I love you if you won't an-swer my

2. call. Are we talk-ing the same lang-uage? May-be I can't read the signs.

D.C. al Coda

Is it good for us to-ge-ther or are we trains on diff-rent lines?

Coda

Some-things matter more than o-thers and you mat-ter most of all.

But I can't tell you that I love you if you won't an-swer my call.

1. **READING STRATEGY**: Understanding figurative language. Read the words of the song. Then circle the answers. You can also listen to the song on the cassette.

1. *Are we talking the same language?* means
   a. Are we both speaking English?
   b. Do we understand each other's feelings?
2. *Signs* in *Maybe I can't read the signs* means
   a. things that people do that show how they feel.
   b. things like road signs and advertising signs.
3. *Maybe your heart's overcrowded, maybe mine's beating out of time* is about
   a. emotional reasons why the two people haven't been getting along very well.
   b. the medical reasons why the two people can't get married.
4. *Wall* in *Maybe there's a wall between us* means
   a. part of a room or building.
   b. something that keeps two people from understanding each other.
5. *Some things matter more than others and you matter most of all* means
   a. I'm worried that you're sick.
   b. You're the most important thing in my life.

2. **READING STRATEGY**: Understanding figurative language.

1. *Are we trains on different lines?*
   Why do you think the songwriter chose to talk about trains and railroad lines? What is he saying here?
2. *Silence is a deadly weapon, killing love. . .*
   What do you understand by "silence"? Do you agree that it kills love?

3. LISTENING. Since their fight in the park, Mac has tried to call Maria several times, but she's never home. Now Mac is talking with his roommate, Larry. Listen to their conversation and circle the answers.

1. When Larry says "If I were you, I'd call her," he is
   a. worried about Maria.
   b. worried about Mac's problem with Maria.
   c. worried about the quotation he wants Maria to translate.
2. When Mac says ". . . Don't worry about it," he is
   a. trying to end the conversation.
   b. trying to make Larry feel better.
   c. trying to make himself feel better.

Why is Mac over at Paula's?
What does Paula suggest about Mac's career plans?
How does Mac like her suggestion?

After his conversation with Larry, Mac called Maria once more. She still wasn't home, so he went next door to Paula's.

"Hi. Are you busy?" he asked when she opened the door.

"No. Come on in."

"I had to get out of the apartment for a while."

"What's the matter?"

"It's Larry. He's driving me crazy. I really think he's the most obnoxious person I've ever met."

"That bad, huh?"

"Yeah, that bad. Just now he wanted me to call Maria because *he* wants her to translate something for him. Then he started asking a lot of questions about Maria and me. I wish he'd mind his own business."

"I see what you mean. That *would* be hard to put up with. I suppose you've let him know how you feel."

"Yeah, but it doesn't do any good. He doesn't pay any attention. Oh, well, school'll be over soon. I guess I can put up with him until then."

"How's your job-hunting going?" asked Paula.

"Well, I don't know if I told you this. I haven't even decided for sure, but I might go into sales instead of engineering."

"No kidding! I thought you wanted to be an engineer."

"I did, but I haven't been able to find a good job and it's getting too late to find anything before school's over."

"Well, if I'd known that, I would've told you to talk to Ray. I bet he could tell you a lot about sales and probably give you some names."

"Yeah, I bet he could.... I wish I'd told you sooner."

"I'll talk to him about it as soon as he gets back. He's in Seattle until next week."

"Thanks. I'd appreciate it," said Mac gratefully.

"What's Maria doing these days?"

"Oh, the same old thing. Actually, I haven't seen her for a couple of days, but I'm going to call her later."

"Oh, could you do me a favor? Could you ask her if she wants to go see *The Rainmaker* next Wednesday?"

"OK. When do you want her to let you know?"

"Oh, just tell her to call me sometime this weekend, all right?"

"Sure."

---

4. CONVERSATION. Complain about someone who bothers you.

A: What's the matter?

B: It's __(name)__. *He's/She's* driving me crazy. I really think *he's/she's the/one of the* _____

A: That bad, huh?

B: Yeah, that bad. *He's/She's always/never* _____. *Just now/The other day* _____.

A: I see what you mean. That would _____. I suppose _____.

B: Yeah, but _____.

You can say:
I really think he's . . .

.. { the most obnoxious person I've ever met.
one of the most inconsiderate people I've ever met.
the most unreasonable boss I've ever had.
one of the hardest teachers I've ever had.
the worst driver/cook /etc. I've ever known.

5.   CONVERSATION

A:

> You have almost decided to make a major change in your plans for work or school.

B:

> A is going to tell you about a change in his/her plans for work or school.

> Tell **B** about your plans:
> *You know, I haven't decided for sure, but I might* .... *instead of* ....

> You're surprised:
> *No kidding! I thought you were going to/ wanted to* ....

> Explain:
> *I was/did, but* ....

> You can say:
>
> ... but { I haven't been able to find a good job.
> It's getting too late to find a job before graduation.
> I was talking to someone who suggested business school.
> I can't do anything until I save some money.

> You know someone who might help **A**. Explain:
> *Well, if I'd known that, I would've/could've*
> ....

> Respond:
> .... *I wish I'd told you sooner.*

6.   CONVERSATION

> **A:**   You're planning to call or see someone that you and **B** know.

> **B:**   A is going to call or see someone you know. Ask **A** to give the person a message.

A: *I might/I'm going to* .... *later.*
B: Oh, could you do me a favor? Could you tell .... *(that) about/to* ....? OR Could you ask .... *if/about/to* ....?
A: OK. When do you want *him/her* to let you know?
B: Oh, *(just)* tell *him/her* to ....
A: Sure.

> You can say:
> Tell him/her to let me know ...
>
> ... { as soon as possible.
> when he gets back from Boston.
> by tomorrow.
> before Sunday.
> after work tomorrow.

7.   WRITING SKILLS. Mac wrote to his parents to tell them he might give up engineering and look for a job in sales.
Write the <u>date, greeting, first and last paragraphs, closing</u> and <u>signature</u> of the letter in the space provided. Remember to indent your paragraphs. Capitalize and punctuate where necessary.

may 5 1980 dear mom and dad howve you been sorry I havent written for a while Ive been really busy for the last couple of weeks with job interviews term papers and getting ready for final exams

I haven't decided for sure yet, but I might try to get a job in sales instead of engineering. I don't think I can get the kind of engineering job I want because of my grades. On the other hand, if I go into sales, I might get a pretty good job where I can use my engineering background.

Before I make up my mind, I need more information. Paula's friend Ray is a sales representative for Western Mining and Manufacturing and she said I should talk to him. I'm going to give him a call next week, so I'll let you know what he says next time I write.

well I realize this is short but Ive got an exam at 900 tomorrow and I havent finished reading the material yet love mac

8.   WRITING SKILLS. Now plan and write two paragraphs like the second and third paragraphs in Mac's letter. Tell a friend about a possible change in your future plans.

- Begin your first paragraph:
  I haven't decided for sure yet, but I might/might not ....
- Begin your second paragraph:
  Before I make up my mind, I need/have to/want to ....

9.   GRAMMAR REVIEW. Paula got a call from her colleague Jack Andropoulos, who wanted to borrow her suitcase to take on his vacation. Fill in each blank with one item from I and one item from II. Items from I may be used more than once.

I	II
that	I told you I was going there
what	works in a travel agency
when	I went to Puerto Rico
where	you were going to Puerto Rico
who	you want
after	it got so popular
before	you could swim and be in the sun
	people kept trying to sell me things on the beach
	I ever took
	I talked to you

PAULA: I didn't know ....
1
I think you'll like it.

JACK: I thought ....
2

PAULA: No, you told me you wanted to go someplace

.... ,
3

but I thought you were thinking about Florida.

JACK: Oh, that's right. I guess I didn't tell you. Well,

.... I was at
4

a friend's house in New Jersey and I met this guy

....
5

and he offered me a fantastic discount.

PAULA: Great. And if sunshine's ....
6
...., you're certainly going to the right

place. One of the nicest vacations ....
7

.... was ....
8
.... Of course,

I was there ....
9

JACK: How were the beaches?

PAULA: Great. The only thing I didn't like was ....
10

....

....

JACK: Yeah, that would get on my nerves too.

Who else is coming over to Maria's?
How well do Maria and Franco like TV?

Maria and Franco just came back from riding their bikes all afternoon. They're at Maria's apartment.

FRANCO: Hey, what about that cake you promised to make?

MARIA: Oh, that's right. Why don't I make it now? Tomiko's coming over later and I was wondering what I could make. I've got a good recipe for lemon cake. Do you like lemon?

FRANCO: That sounds fine to me. Can I help?

MARIA: No, that's OK. Why don't you turn on the TV?

FRANCO: No, I don't watch TV very much—only when I don't have anything else to do. There's never anything good on anymore.

MARIA: Oh, I watch it once in a while. There are a few programs I like.

10. FORM. Maria and Franco are continuing their conversation. Follow the instructions in parentheses and write Franco's part of the conversation. Then practice it with a partner.

MARIA: Hey, did you use to watch "Bonanza"?

FRANCO: Sure. ....
    1.(It used to be Franco's favorite show.)

MARIA: What ever happened to the guy who played the oldest son?

FRANCO: You mean ....?
    2.(Franco thinks Maria's talking

....
about the tall, heavyset guy with the big smile.)

MARIA: No, that was the second son. The one I mean wasn't as tall. He was dark and good-looking and he always wore black. He left the show after the first year or so.

FRANCO: ....
    3.(Franco knows who she means, but he doesn't

....
remember his name.)

MARIA: Oh, I always thought he was so handsome. I really liked the show when he was on. . . . Have you seen him in anything lately?

FRANCO: No, ...
    4.(Franco hasn't seen him in anything

....
since he was on "Bonanza.")

From the television series "BONANZA"
Courtesy of NBC Enterprises

From the television series "...
Cou...

11. CONVERSATION. Talk about a TV performer that you used to like. Begin like this:

A: What ever happened to the :............... who ....?

> *Ask about a performer like this:*
> What ever happened to the . . .
> . . . { guy **who played** the oldest son on "Bonanza"?
>   woman **who used to be** on "Laugh-In"?

Who called?
What did he call for?
What was Maria going to say
before she had to hang up?

Maria finished mixing the cake and put it in the oven.

FRANCO: Hey, Maria, could I have a cup of coffee?

MARIA: Oh, gee, Franco, I don't have any—I forgot to buy some.

FRANCO: Would you like me to go get some?

MARIA: Do you mind?

FRANCO: No. Where can I get it around here?

MARIA: There's a store on Charles Street. That's probably the closest place.

FRANCO: OK. Want to come with me?

MARIA: No, I can't leave until the cake's done.

FRANCO: OK. How do I get there?

MARIA: When you walk out of the building, turn left and walk to Sullivan Street. Turn right on Sullivan and walk to the next corner. That's West Third Street. Turn left and it's right there—almost on the corner.

FRANCO: OK. Be back in a little while.

While Franco was gone, the telephone rang.

MARIA: Hello?

MAC: Maria. How've you been?

MARIA: Oh, Mac. . . . I'm fine. How've *you* been?

MAC: Fine. Busy. . . . Where've you been? I've been trying to call you and you're never home.

MARIA: Oh. Well, I—I haven't been home much. How's George doing?

MAC: Much better, thanks. He says his ribs don't hurt much anymore, so he can use crutches now and move around a little.

MARIA: Well, that's good. Is he home yet?

MAC: Yeah, he came home a few days ago.

MARIA: I know how he must feel. I broke my leg once too. Do you know how much longer he'll have to wear a cast?

MAC: Probably for another eight weeks. It was a pretty bad break.

MARIA: Eight weeks! By then he'll be going crazy. Anyway, I'm glad he's home now.

MAC: Yeah, so's he. Listen, honey, I want to apologize for the other day. I wasn't very nice. Are you still mad?

MARIA: No, Mac. I'm not mad. And it was my fault too, but—Oh, darn, there's the doorbell. It's probably Tomiko. Look, I'll call you back later, OK?

MAC: Uh—yeah—all right. I'll be here.

MARIA: Bye.

MAC: Bye.

12.   DISCUSSION. Talk about Mac and Maria with two or three other people. Here are some things you can discuss:

- What do you know about Mac and Maria so far? What do you know about Franco?
- What do you think Maria *should* do now? What do you think she *will* do?
- Will Maria and Mac get back together again?

13.   CONVERSATION. Tell someone where to find something and how to get there.

A: Where can I *find/get* .... around here?
B: Well, there's .... on .... That's probably the closest *place/one.*
A: OK. Want to come with me?
B: No, I can't leave until ....
A: OK. How do I get there?
B: ....

> *If the directions are complicated, you can check to be sure you understand:*
>
> B: OK, let me see if I've got that right. I ....
> A: That's right.   OR   No, you ....

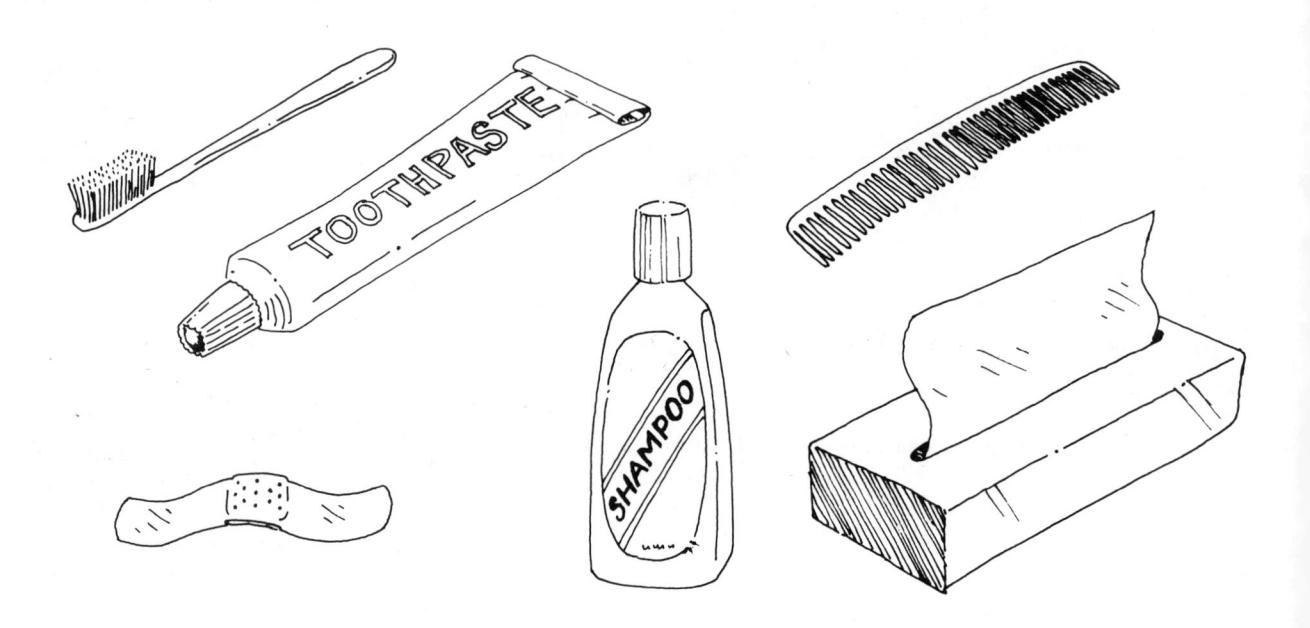

14.   CONVERSATION. Ask about someone who was sick or injured.

A: How's .... doing?
B: Much better, thanks. *He/She* says .... anymore.   OR   Not so well yet. *He/She* says .... still ....
A: .... Do you know how much longer .... ?
B: Probably *for/until* ....
A: .... ! By then *he'll/she'll* .... Anyway, I'm *glad/sorry* ....   OR   Oh, well, that's not too long. Anyway, I'm *glad/sorry* ....
B: ....

15.   GRAMMAR REVIEW. Franco got back from the store soon after Tomiko arrived. Maria made some coffee and cut the cake. Fill in the blanks with items from the list. You will have to use some of the items more than once.

a	any	one of the	such	to
an	big	some	than	too
another	bigger	some more	the	

MARIA: Well, who's ready for .... _1_ cake?

TOMIKO: Me, but just .... _2_ small piece, please. No, that's .... _3_ big.

MARIA: OK. Here's one that isn't as .... _4_. Franco? How about you?

FRANCO: I'd like a .... _5_ piece .... _6_ Tomiko's, please. I've been looking forward to this cake.

MARIA: Coffee?

FRANCO: Yes, please.

TOMIKO: Mmm. I'll have a cup too.

MARIA: Here you are. Watch out. It's still .... _7_ hot .... _8_ drink. Sugar?

FRANCO: No, thanks.

TOMIKO: Do you have .... _9_ milk?—that's OK. Don't get up. I'll get it.

MARIA: There's .... _10_ open carton in .... _11_ refrigerator. Use that one first.

FRANCO: Hey, this is .... _12_ best cakes I've ever tasted. I didn't know you were .... _13_ a good cook.

MARIA: Thank you. It's a good recipe, isn't it?

TOMIKO: It really is good, Maria.

MARIA: Thanks. . . . Franco, are you ready for .... _14_ coffee?

FRANCO: Sure, I'll have .... _15_ cup.

16.   GRAMMAR REVIEW. Franco checked the different TV channels to see if there was anything worth watching. Complete the sentences with one of the phrases beneath each TV screen.

> If ....,
> I never would've hired you.

a. I'll know about you
b. I know about you
c. I'd known about you

> So if .... your dishes really
> clean, use new Zap dishwashing liquid.

a. you want
b. you'll want
c. you wanted

> Sorry, honey, but if this headache doesn't go away
> pretty soon, I ....able to go.

a. won't be
b. wouldn't be
c. wouldn't have been

> If you want more information about how you can
> build a neighborhood playground, ...
> .... your city park and playground association.

a. you should call
b. you should've called
c. you called

17. **Complete the conversation and say it with a partner.**

PAULA: What's there to do in ....

  besides ....?

YOU: Well, you really should ....

  ....

  And if ...., be sure to

  ....

PAULA: Is there ....

  to/where ....?

YOU: Well, there's a ....

  in/on/near...

PAULA: Is there anything else worth...

  ....?

YOU: ....

  ....

You've Learned To

UNIT 1

start a conversation:	Hi, Paula. How are you? OK. So what's new with *you*?
emphasize:	Well, as a matter of fact, I *do* have something to tell you.
talk about a decision:	I've decided to go back to school./I'm going back to school. Really? Why? Because I need to know something about retailing. Have you decided where you want to go? No, not yet, but I've been thinking about Fordham.
report a conversation:	I was just talking to Maggie. She said she's decided to go back to school.
ask for further information:	Did she tell you what she wants to study?/What else did she have to say?
make a suggestion:	How about Fordham? From what I've heard, it has one of the best programs around here for returning students.
invite someone to do something:	I'm having a surprise party for my boyfriend tonight. Why don't you come?
ask for and give directions:	Where is it? 688 Columbus, at 94th St. I live in Greenwich Village. What's the best way to get there? Take the Seventh Avenue subway and get off at 96th Street.
ask someone to repeat something:	What was the address again?

UNIT 2

talk about something that you don't have:	I wish I had my camera so I could take your picture.
offer to lend something:	I've got a camera you can use. I'll get it for you.
make a suggestion:	I think Paula has a camera. Why don't you ask her if you can use it?
ask for information:	Do you know anybody who's looking for a place to live?
identify and describe people:	Larry Allen? He was in our statistics class last spring. Tall, skinny guy? Big nose?
talk about sickness:	What's the matter? Don't you feel well? No, I've got a sore throat and I ache all over. I must be getting a cold or something.
ask who something belongs to:	Do you know whose glasses these are?
talk about probability:	They might be George's. He was sitting here before.
state a conclusion:	They must be Bob's. He has a pair like that.

UNIT 3

apologize and give bad news:	I'm sorry, but I don't think we'll be able to offer you a position.
ask for an explanation:	Could you tell me why not?
ask about a possible solution:	What if I do well on my final exams?
avoid committing yourself:	I really couldn't say, but it might be worth a try. Maybe we can go some other time. That's an interesting idea.

make a suggestion:	Have you ever considered a career in sales?/Why don't you think about it?
encourage:	Don't let it get you down. You'll get a job.
invite someone to do something:	Are you doing anything this evening? I was thinking of going to see *All That Jazz*.
reject an invitation:	I'd love to, but I have to study.
suggest an alternative:	How about tomorrow?
reject a suggestion:	That's an interesting idea. I think I'd rather stay in engineering, though.
talk about something that happened recently:	I just got fired.
express regret:	I wish I'd studied harder these last few months.

UNIT 4

identify something:	Which one? The one with the article about women journalists.
make, agree to and refuse requests:	Do you mind if I borrow it? Of course not. I'll bring it tomorrow./Sorry, I'm using it right now. Would you bring us some more butter, please?/Could I have another fork? Sure.
start a business telephone conversation:	Paula Duran. Ms. Duran, my name's Marilyn Dixon. Jack Andropoulos suggested that I call you.
offer to help:	How can I help you?
extend and accept an invitation:	I was wondering if we could have lunch sometime this week. OK.
ask for suggestions:	Where would you like to meet?/Can you suggest a place?
make, accept and reject suggestions:	How about the Red Onion on West 39th Street? Fine. Would you care to order a drink before lunch?/Something to drink? Yes, please./Not right now, thank you.
take an order and order in a restaurant:	Are you ready to order? I'd like roast beef, but no potato, please. How would you like your roast beef? Medium. Will there be anything else? Not right now, thanks.
confirm an appointment:	I'll see you there on Thursday at one o'clock.
identify someone:	Are you Paula Duran? You must be Marilyn Dixon.

UNIT 6

ask someone to repeat something:	What's the name of the place again?
ask for and give directions:	How do I get there? When you leave the station, turn left. Walk two blocks and turn right. I don't remember the name of the street, but there's a bank on the corner.
ask for and give confirmation:	OK, let me see if I've got that right. I turn right at the bank? That's right.
make a request:	Let me get a pencil. Wait a minute.

talk about how someone's feeling:	How are you feeling?/How are you doing?
	Much better. My leg doesn't hurt too much anymore.
	Not too well. My ribs still hurt.
	Well, I'm glad you're OK.
talk about an accident:	How did it happen anyway?
	I was checking some work on the second story and I slipped and fell.
	You're lucky you weren't killed.
ask if someone has done something:	Have you talked to Mom and Dad yet?
ask about and report a conversation:	What did they say?
	They didn't seem too upset. They said I should've been more careful.
talk about how long something will continue:	How long are you going to be in the hospital?
	Probably until Wednesday./Not too long, I hope.

UNIT 7

make a request:	Could you do me a favor? Could you stay until nine tonight?
refuse a request, but offer to do something else to help:	Gee, I'm sorry I can't. But I might be able to stay until seven thirty, if that's any help.
accept the offer:	Yeah, that would help.
refuse the offer:	No, I'm afraid it wouldn't. But thanks anyway.
ask someone to wait for an answer:	I'll let you know for sure as soon as I make a phone call.
leave a message:	Could you give Mac a message for me? Ask him to bring my umbrella.
express concern:	What happened? I was getting worried.
ask for clarification:	What message?
	What do you mean?
report what happened:	I called to tell you I'd be late. Larry promised to leave you a note.
complain about someone:	Larry's really been getting on my nerves. He's such a slob and he's so inconsiderate.
sympathize:	That'd drive me crazy too.
make a suggestion:	I suppose you've already told him how you feel./Have you tried saying no?/Have you thought about asking him to leave?/Have you talked to him about it?
accept the suggestion:	It might be worth a try.
express resignation:	I guess I'll just have to put up with it.

UNIT 8

express impatience:	I'm getting hungry. How much longer are you going to be?
	Oh, an hour and a half.
	An hour and a half? By then it'll be too late to go to a movie or anything.
apologize and explain:	I'm sorry, but I can't stop until I finish going over my notes.
complain to someone about his/her behavior:	I wish you'd told me you were going to study all day. I thought we were going out.
defend yourself:	Come on. You knew I had to study.
say what you would have done, but didn't do:	If I'd known, I would've make plans to do something else.

talk about someone you used to know:	Do you ever hear from Tony?
	Yeah. I got a letter from him last week. He's fine. He's running his family's restaurant now.
	What ever happened to that tall African woman who looked like a model? Is she still around?
	I don't know. I haven't seen her since the course was over.
ask for confirmation:	You mean Jeannette Kaba?

UNIT 9

talk about a movie:	That was a good movie, wasn't it?
	Yeah, it was. I thought the best part was when Lois Lane found out Clark Kent was Superman.
	Yeah, but wasn't it sad when he had to give up his powers so he could marry her?
talk about something you didn't like:	Actually, the only thing I didn't like was when those three outlaws destroyed that small town. It was so violent.
talk about an actor/actress:	Wasn't Christopher Reeve good?
	And he's so handsome.
	He played this writer who fell in love with a woman who lived a long time ago.
compare:	I thought he was even better in *Somewhere in Time.*/I didn't think he was as good in *Somewhere in Time.*
talk about future plans:	Where are you going for vacation?
	We haven't decided yet, but I want to go somewhere with lots of sun.
make a suggestion:	If that's what you're looking for, you should go to Fort Lauderdale.
	You can always go to Miami. If you do, be sure to go to Dino's.
object to the suggestion:	Won't it be too hot by then?
ask for further information:	What's there to do besides lie on the beach? Are there any tours worth taking?

Grammar Index

Irregular Verbs

Base Form*	Past Tense	Past Participle
be	was/were	been
beat	beat	beaten
become	became	become
begin	began	begun
bend	bent	bent
bet	bet	bet
bite	bit	bitten
blow	blew	blown
break	broke	broken
bring	brought	brought
build	built	built
buy	bought	bought
catch	caught	caught
choose	chose	chosen
come	came	come
cost	cost	cost
cut	cut	cut
dig	dug	dug
do	did	done
draw	drew	drawn
drink	drank	drunk
drive	drove	driven
eat	ate	eaten
fall	fell	fallen
feed	fed	fed
feel	felt	felt
fight	fought	fought
find	found	found
fit	fit	fit
fly	flew	flown
forget	forgot	forgotten
freeze	froze	frozen
get	got	gotten
give	gave	given
go	went	gone
hang	hung	hung
have	had	had
hear	heard	heard
hide	hid	hidden
hit	hit	hit
hold	held	held
hurt	hurt	hurt
keep	kept	kept
know	knew	known
lay	laid	laid
lead	led	led
leave	left	left
lend	lent	lent

Base Form*	Past Tense	Past Participle
let	let	let
lie	lay	lain
light	lit	lit
lose	lost	lost
make	made	made
mean	meant	meant
meet	met	met
put	put	put
quit	quit	quit
read	read	read
ride	rode	ridden
ring	rang	rung
rise	rose	risen
run	ran	run
say	said	said
see	saw	seen
sell	sold	sold
send	sent	sent
set	set	set
shake	shook	shaken
shine	shone	shone
shoot	shot	shot
shut	shut	shut
sing	sang	sung
sink	sank	sunk
sit	sat	sat
sleep	slept	slept
slide	slid	slid
speak	spoke	spoken
spend	spent	spent
stand	stood	stood
steal	stole	stolen
stick	stuck	stuck
strike	struck	struck
swear	swore	sworn
sweep	swept	swept
swim	swam	swum
take	took	taken
teach	taught	taught
tear	tore	torn
tell	told	told
think	thought	thought
throw	threw	thrown
understand	understood	understood
wake	woke	woke/woken
wear	wore	worn
win	won	won
write	wrote	written

*infinitive = to + base form (to be, to give, etc.)

Word List

The page number beside each word tells you where the word first appears in the book. This Word List does not include words that first appeared in Student's Book 1.

A

absent 27
absolute 95
accident 56
accidental 58
accidentally 72
ache (v) 16
according to 58
accounting 26
acre 7
act (v) 83
action 19
active 23
actor 90
actress 90
added (adj.) 97
administer 58
admit 51
advance (v) 42
advanced (adj.) 30
advancement 30
adviser 51
affluent 81
afterward 57
against 58
agree on 54
agreeable 19
aid (n) 4
aim (v) 51
alcohol 18
alternative (n) 32
although 18
amateur (n) 30
ambition 51
ambulance 67
among 81
amount 36
amusing (adj.) 97
ankle 64
anniversary 97
announcer 31
annoyed (adj.) 69
annually 18
anymore 62
anytime 97
appetizer 40
approach (v) 95
approximately 18
arithmetic 73
arrival 57
artificial 58
ashtray 44
aside 18
aspect 73
aspiration 81
assignment 42
assist 30
assistance 4
associate (n) 42
association 108
assume 47
assure 82
at any rate 69
athletic 57

B

athletics 23
attendance 25
attract 4
audiovisual 48
authentic 94
authority 51
authorization 65
authorize 65
auto 61
availability 29
average (adj.) 18
average (n) 18
avoid 28
award (v) 4
award-winning 97
aware 56
awfully 2

baby sitter 31
baccarat 95
back (n) 63
background 24
backyard 19
bacon 40
badly 58
baked (adj.) 40
balance 65
ballroom 48
banker 19
banking 26
banquet 48
baseline 57
basic 58
basically 24
bathroom 16
bathtub 75
battle 88
beard 15
beaver 95
beef 18
belong 17
beneath 108
best seller 72
beverage 40
big-horn 95
bike (n) 50
bilingual 30
biologist 33
biology 26
birth 65
bit 18
blackjack 95
bleed 58
bleeding (n) 58
blind (adj.) 51
blind (n) 51
blood 58
bluefish 40
blues 28
board (n) 72
boatman 95
body 23

bombing (n) 42
bonanza 36
bond 57
bookkeeper 47
boom 81
boss 19
bother 75
bounce (v) 57
Boy Scout 31
branch 58
bread 39
break (n) 1
break (v) 51
breathe 16
breathing (n) 57
breeze 30
brick 61
brief 51
broke (break) 51
broken (break) 59
bungalow 72
burden 72
bureau 51
busboy 30
butter (n) 39
butter (v) 39
by heart 51

C

cake 8
calendar 37
call in 69
camera 13
camp (n) 30
camping (n) 95
campus 7
candidate 30
candy 91
cannon ball 98
cap 57
capitalize 102
cappuccino 91
cardiac arrest 58
cardiopulmonary resuscitation
   (cpr) 57
care (v) 40
carefree 80
carefully 65
carrot 39
carton 107
case 18
casino 95
casserole 18
cassette 36
cast 62
caught (catch) 72
cause (v) 19
celebrate 97
celebration 94
Census Bureau 4
century 72
certificate 56
challenge (n) 53

Chamber of Commerce 94
changeable 73
channel 108
charge (v) 72
charge card 18
charm 89
checkout (n) 48
checklist 36
chemistry 26
chest 57
chew 57
chicken 19
chills 16
chip 95
choice 36
chose (choose) 99
cigar 90
circuit 98
circumstance 7
citizen 18
civil 81
claim (n) 65
claim (v) 19
clarification 60
clean up 75
clear (v) 57
clerical 30
cloth 58
cloud 81
clue 73
cocktail 40
coffee shop 70
cold (n) 16
coldly 78
colleague 103
combine (v) 57
combined (adj.) 18
comedy 97
comfort (n) 4
commit 132
community 59
companion 94
comparison 7
competitive 30
compile 18
complete (adj.) 53
complete (v) 68
complicated (adj.) 51
compose 88
compression 57
compulsive 75
computer 26
computer programmer 26
computerized (adj.) 47
concern (n) 76
concerned (adj.) 16
conclusion 20
conduct (v) 88
cone 91
confirm 9
confront 88
confrontation 81
congested (adj.) 16
congratulations 49

slumping (*adj.*) 18
smiling (*adj.*) 72
smoothly 53
snap (*v*) 35
sneeze 16
soak 58
social 31
Social Security 81
social worker 26
sociology 80
sofa 17
solution 19
someday 72
somehow 62
songwriter 99
sooner or later 27
sore 16
sort of 89
sound (*n*) 72
sound track 88
source 81
southeast 30
southern 94
spa 30
spaghetti 18
speaker 73
specify 23
spectacular 95
spinach 39
sportswriting 42
spouse 81
square (*n*) 50
squeeze 19
stagger 57
stairs 19
stand up 24
stardust 94
state (*n*) 73
state (*v*) 19
statistically 18
statistics 15
statue 94
steadily 19
steel 88
steer (*n*) 19
stenographer 72
stew 40
stock (*n*) 94
stomach 16
stomachache 16
stop (*n*) 51
story 59
straight 15
strangely 81
streamlined 48
stress (*n*) 81
stricken 57
strike (*n*) 57
strike (*v*) 58
striking (*adj.*) 72
string beans 45
strong 58

succeeding (*adj.*) 81
studies (*n*) 30
stuff (*n*) 62
stuffed up (*adj.*) 16
substitute (*v*) 30
suburb 19
suburban 18
subscription 36
such as 19
sudden 19
suddenly 19
sugar 107
sunbathing (*n*) 95
sunshine 103
super 97
superlative 11
supervisor 29
support (*n*) 81
support (*v*) 81
supposed 39
supremacy 88
supremely 51
surface 58
surprising (*adj.*) 58
survey 80
suspect 58
suit (*v*) 95
suitable 88
swallow (*v*) 18
sweepstakes 94
switchboard 72
symbol 23
sympathetically 62
sympathize 34

T

tablet 16
take care of 4
take out 18
take a walk 91
talk (*n*) 55
tape 88
tart 40
taste (*v*) 107
taught (teach) 57
tea 40
Technicolor 88
temperature 22
tend 81
tense 72
terror 95
test (*v*) 30
themselves 23
thick 58
thin 15
throat 16
throw 58
thrown out (throw out) 27
thumb 19
timed (*adj.*) 51
times (*n*) 72
toast 40

tobacco 57
toe 64
tolerate 58
tool 23
top 30
topic 42
total 18
toward 81
track (*n*) 60
traditional 4
tragic 59
train (*v*) 30
trainer 57
training (*adj.*) 67
transit 50
translate 99
translation 48
translater 26
trauma 81
travel (*n*) 51
traveler 51
treat 65
trend 81
truly 11
try (*n*) 24
tuition 7
turn down 27
turkey 40
twisted (*adj.*) 98
type (*n*) 63
type (*v*) 30
typing (*n*) 30

U

umpire (*n*) 57
umpire (*v*) 57
unaided (*adj.*) 51
uncomplimentary 15
unconscious 57
undergraduate (*adj.*) 7
undergraduate (*n*) 7
understood (understand) 79
unfriendly 11
unhappily 78
unkind 81
unlimited 95
unlock 13
unmarried 81
unmotivated 23
unpopular 81
unrealistic 81
unreasonable 75
upset (*v*) 16
upsetting (*adj.*) 34
uptown 50
upward 81
upwards 51
urban 81
use (*n*) 95

V

valid 65

value (*n*) 4
various 18
vegetable 40
vehicle 19
veterinarian 26
victim 58
vocational 4
voice (*n*) 30

W

wages (*n*) 19
waiting (*adj.*) 48
wall 98
want ad 50
war 42
waste (*v*) 2
waterfall 95
wave (*v*) 83
weakly 62
weapon 98
weekly 28
weigh 18
weight 18
weird 98
weird-looking 15
welcoming (*adj.*) 51
welfare 4
well-being 81
well-done 40
westbound 51
western 19
whatever 58
whether 23
whisper (*v*) 13
whose 16
widow 72
widower 1
wilderness 94
wildlife 95
willing 30
winnings 95
wipe 13
wish (*n*) 42
won (win) 31
workday 18
working (*adj.*) 51
workplace 58
world-famous 94
worse 63
worst 6
worth 24
would-be 58
wound (*n*) 58
wrist 64
write down 8
writer 28
writing (*n*) 26
written (write) 56

Y

yacht 95
yank 72

We wish to thank the following for providing us with photographs:

Front Cover—family mechanic, office party, skaters, students, picnic, construction workers: **Dorien Grunbaum.** Baseball players, swing, postman: **Redmond Johnston.** Back Cover—spinner, class painters: **Redmond Johnston.** Page 4, man and children: **Anne Darling;** logger: **Frank Jensen/Monkmeyer Press.** Page 7: **Beaver Boyar Adv./Fordham University.** Page 13: **Ross O'Loughlin.** Page 17, pharmacy: **Dorien Grunbaum;** items: **Ross O'Loughlin.** Page 18, the Pepples at home; near car: **Lee Balterman/PEOPLE Weekly;** Mrs. Pepples teaching class; in laundry room: **Stanley Tretick/PEOPLE Weekly.** Page 23, artist: **Ken Karp;** fishermen: **David Warren/U.S. Department of Agriculture;** scientists: **H. Armstrong Roberts;** carpenters: **Fred S. Witte/U.S. Department of Agriculture;** farmer: **Michelle Bogre/U.S. Department of Agriculture;** engineer: **Ken Karp;** veterinarian: **Tony Maniello/Animal Medical Center.** Page 25, left: **H. Armstrong Roberts;** right: **Ken Karp.** Page 36, Stereo News: **Jon Fein;** Sports Report: **The San Francisco Giants;** Teen Digest: **Jon Fein;** News in Review: **National Archives;** Cycle: **Phil Fein/Monkmeyer Press;** Modern Homemaker: **Mimi Forsyth/Monkmeyer Press;** Fashion: **H. Armstrong Roberts.** Page 45: **Dorien Grunbaum.** Page 46: **Ken Karp.** Page 56: **Louis Psihoyos.** Page 57: **Anne Griffiths/National Geographic Society.** Page 60: **Sarah Van Ouwerkerk.** Pages 71 and 72: **Ross O'Loughlin.** Page 81: **David S. Strickler/Monkmeyer Press.** Page 90, bus: **Greyhound Lines, Inc.;** *Somewhere in Time:* **Universal City Studios;** *Superman II:* **DC Comics Inc.** Page 94, top: **Y. Negata/United Nations;** bottom: **Mark Woodbury.** Page 95, top left: **Las Vegas News Bureau;** bottom left: **Adventure Bound, Inc.;** top right: **Washington Convention and Visitors Assoc.;** Page 104, "Bonanza": **NBC Enterprises;** "Kojak": **MCA Television.** Page 108, top left: **United Artists;** bottom left, top right: **Ken Karp;** bottom right: **H. Armstrong Roberts.**

We wish to thank the following artists:

Pasteup: **Hannah Alderfer.** Page 14: **Anna Veltfort.** Page 16: **Janet Lampart.** Page 21: **M.J. Quay.** Pages 34 and 42: **Tom Leamon.** Pages 63 and 64: **Stuart Leeds.** Page 67: **Anna Veltfort.** Page 68: **Tom Leamon.** Page 106: **Anna Veltfort.**

We wish to thank the following for allowing us to take photographs.

Page 25: **Fountain Restaurant.** Page 47: **Roosevelt Hotel.** Pages 59 and 62: **The Hospital for Special Surgery, N.Y., N.Y.** Page 108: **The Royalton Hotel, 44 W 44 St, N.Y., N.Y. 10036**

Ex 1,3,5 #8
Workbook
)
16